Breck and the Online Troll

Written by Mark Harrington

Illustrated by Eve Yarnton

Salamander Street

First published in 2021 0by Salamander Street Ltd.
(info@salamanderstreet.com)

ISBN: 9781913630706

Printed and bound in Great Britain

10 9 8 7 6 5 4 3 2 1

Contents

About the Breck Foundation

The Breck Foundation is a charity founded by Lorin LaFave after her 14-year old son, Breck Bednar, was groomed online and murdered.

Breck and his friends were groomed by an 18-year-old year old who ran an internet gaming server. They were told an elaborate web of lies to gain their trust. Despite many attempts to stop her son from contacting the predator, and to alert him to the fact that he was being groomed, Lorin was unable to prevent her son's murder in February 2014.

As a result of this tragedy, Lorin founded the Breck Foundation, determined that no other family should have to go through the same ordeal. The charity now delivers powerful presentations using Breck's story as an example; last year it reached more than 16,000 students, 2,000 parents and 4,000 safeguarding professionals.

Lorin believes that had her son seen the kind of talk that the foundation now presents to schools, he would still be alive today.

The foundation wants to ensure that no child is harmed through grooming and exploitation while enjoying their time on the internet. Prevention through education is essential.

The charity's 'play virtual, live real' motto reminds everyone to never meet alone in a private place with someone they have met only online.

For further information and resources, please visit **www.breckfoundation.org.**

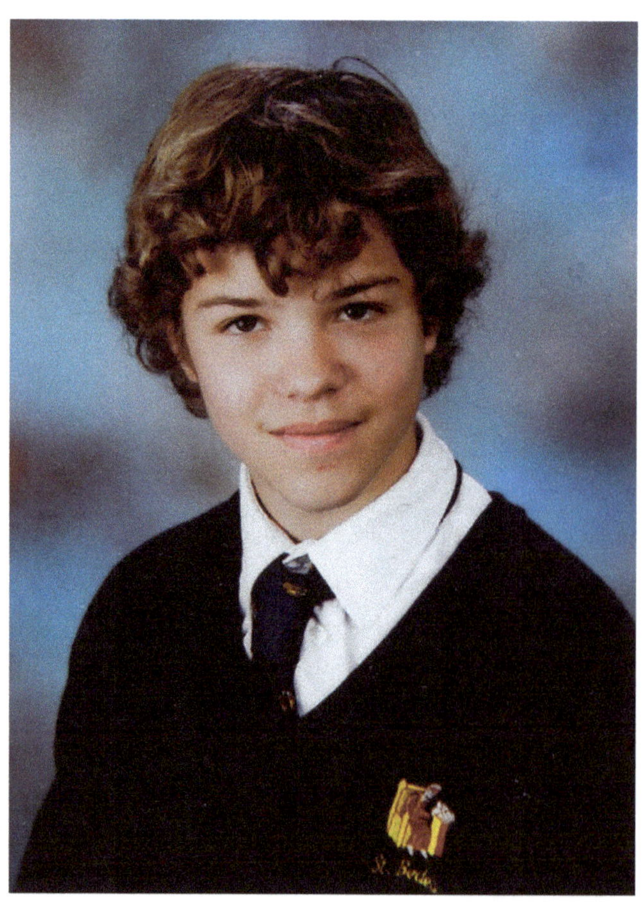

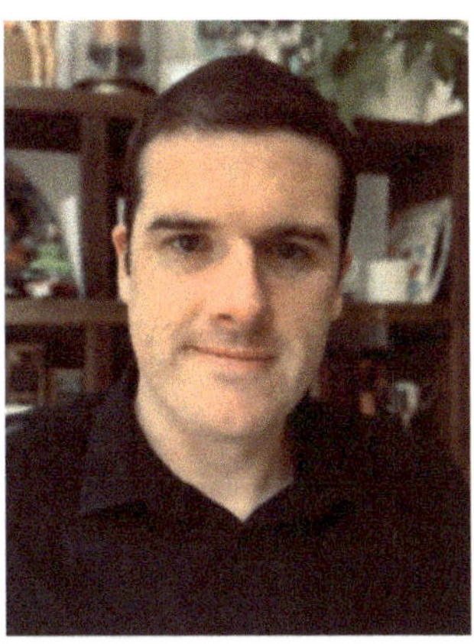

About the Author, Mark Harrington

Mark Harrington is a special needs teacher with more than 10 years' experience in SEN education. He specialises in Drama and English adaptions for special needs education. Mark is a trustee for the Breck Foundation, developing educational resources for the charity. For further projects that Mark is working on please see Instagram @harrington_projects.

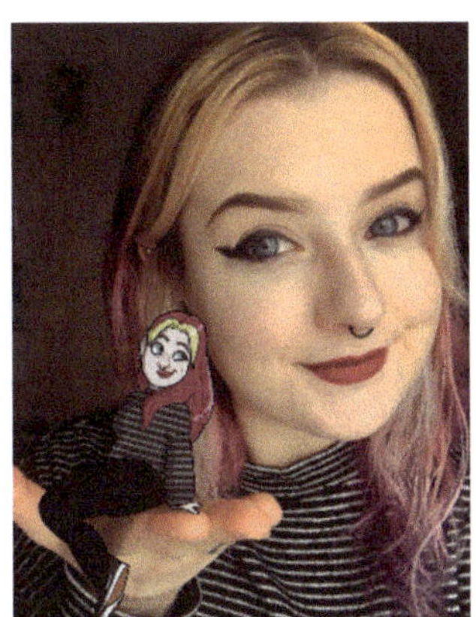

About the illustrator, Eve Yarnton

Eve Yarnton is a digital artist and traditional portrait illustrator from Crawley, England. She has been commissioned for an array of projects varying from album cover art to family portraits, and has aspirations to write her own series of graphic novels. Find Eve on Instagram (evey.ya; eveyarntonart) or contact her at eveyarnton@yahoo.com.

BRECK AND THE ONLINE TROLL

For

Emma, Minnie and Dorothy

&

In memory of Breck Bednar

Once upon a time, there was a young knight called Breck.

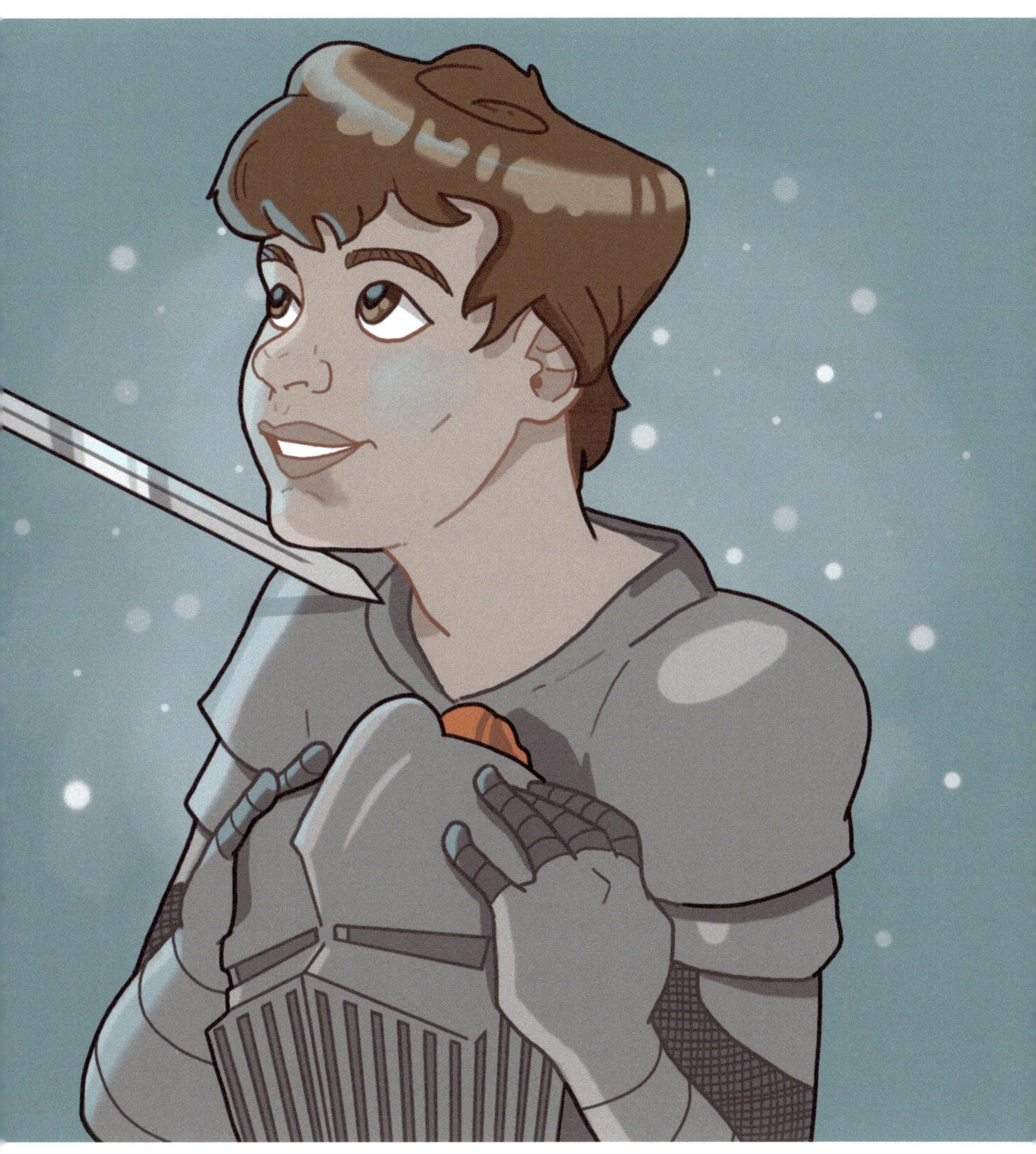

Breck and his group of loyal knights used to enjoy epic quests fighting evil and saving damsels in distress.

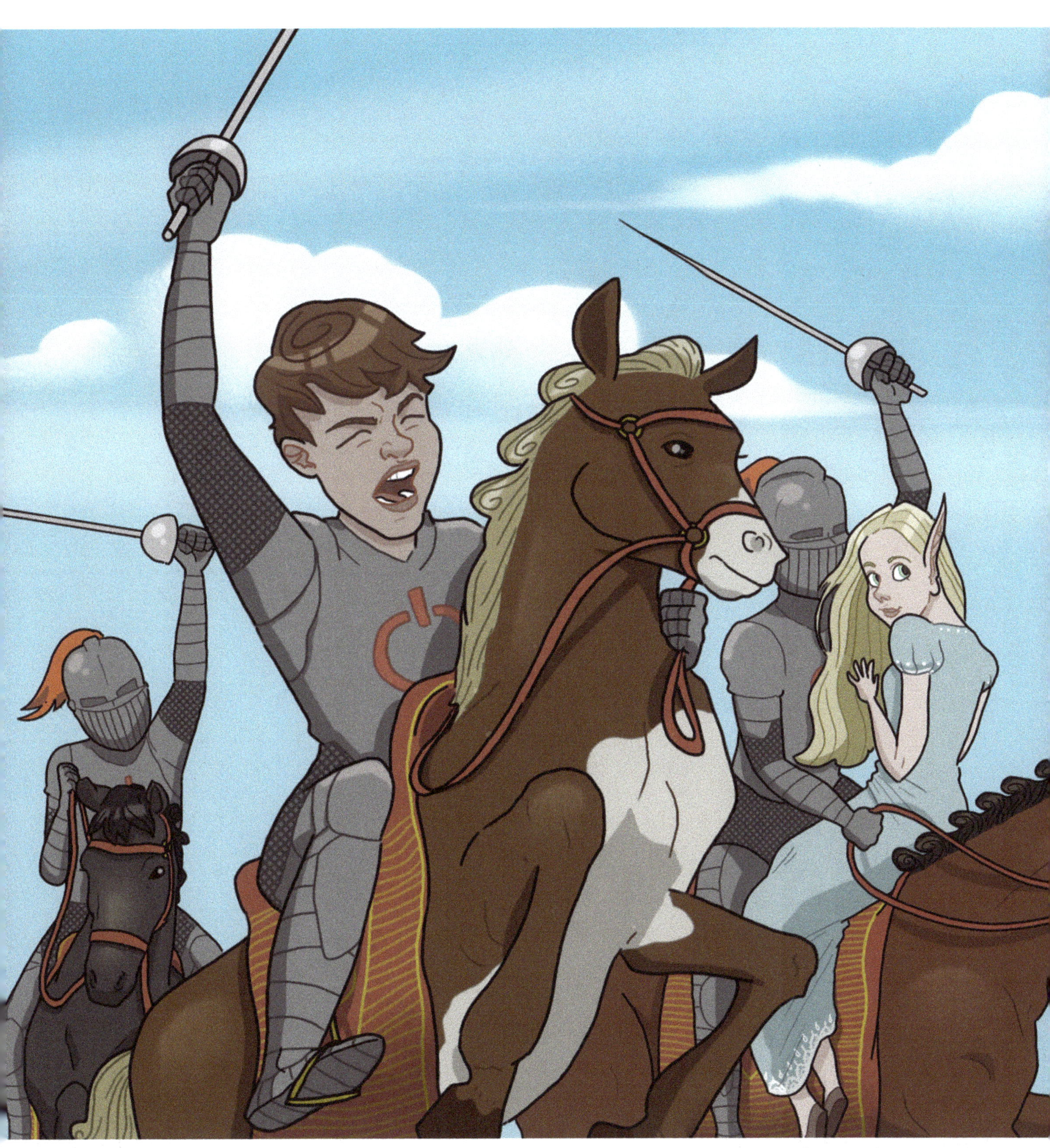

One day the young prince and knights came across a troll.

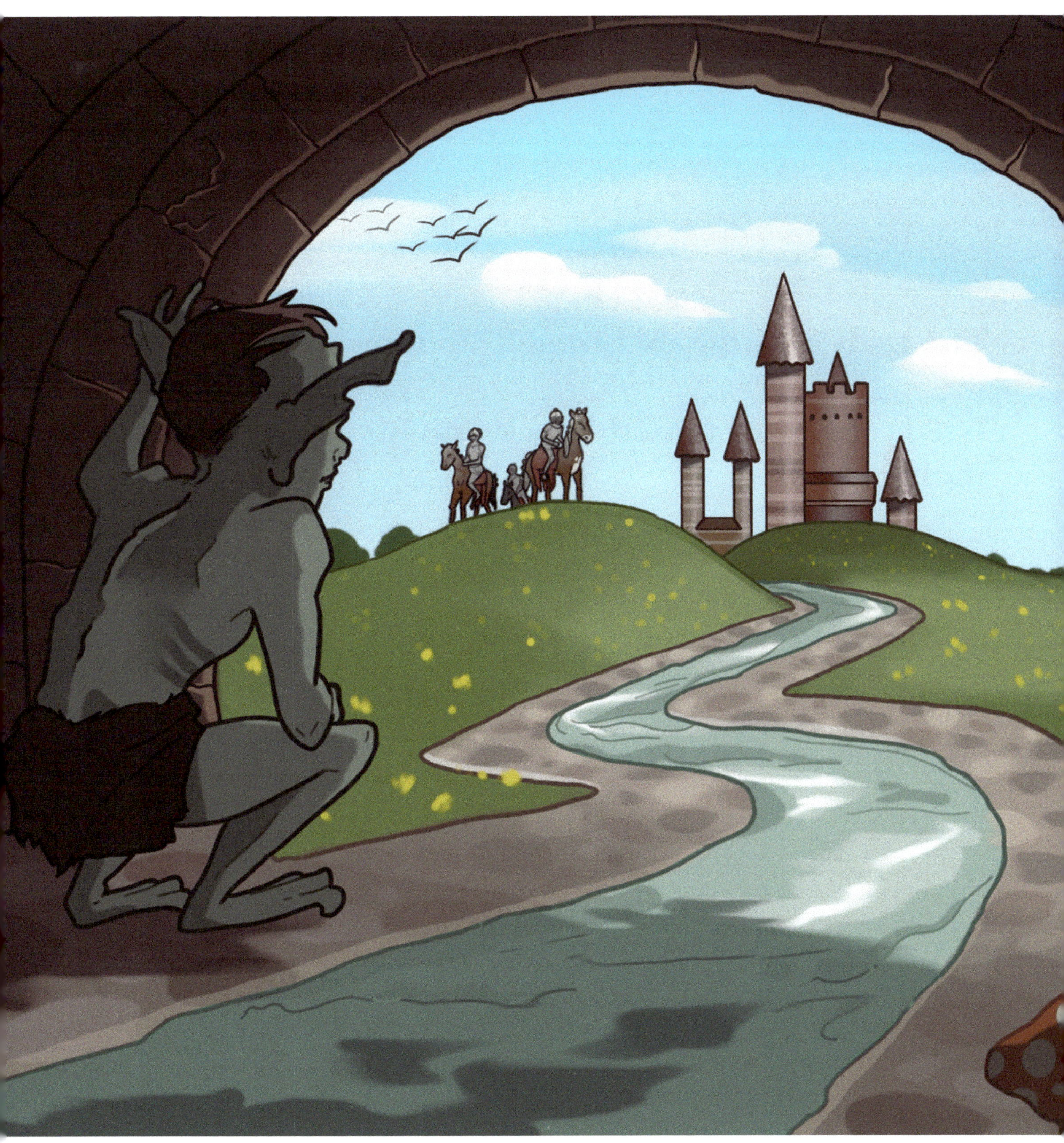

The troll introduced himself as Lewis.

Lewis the Troll joined Breck and his loyal knights on their quests.

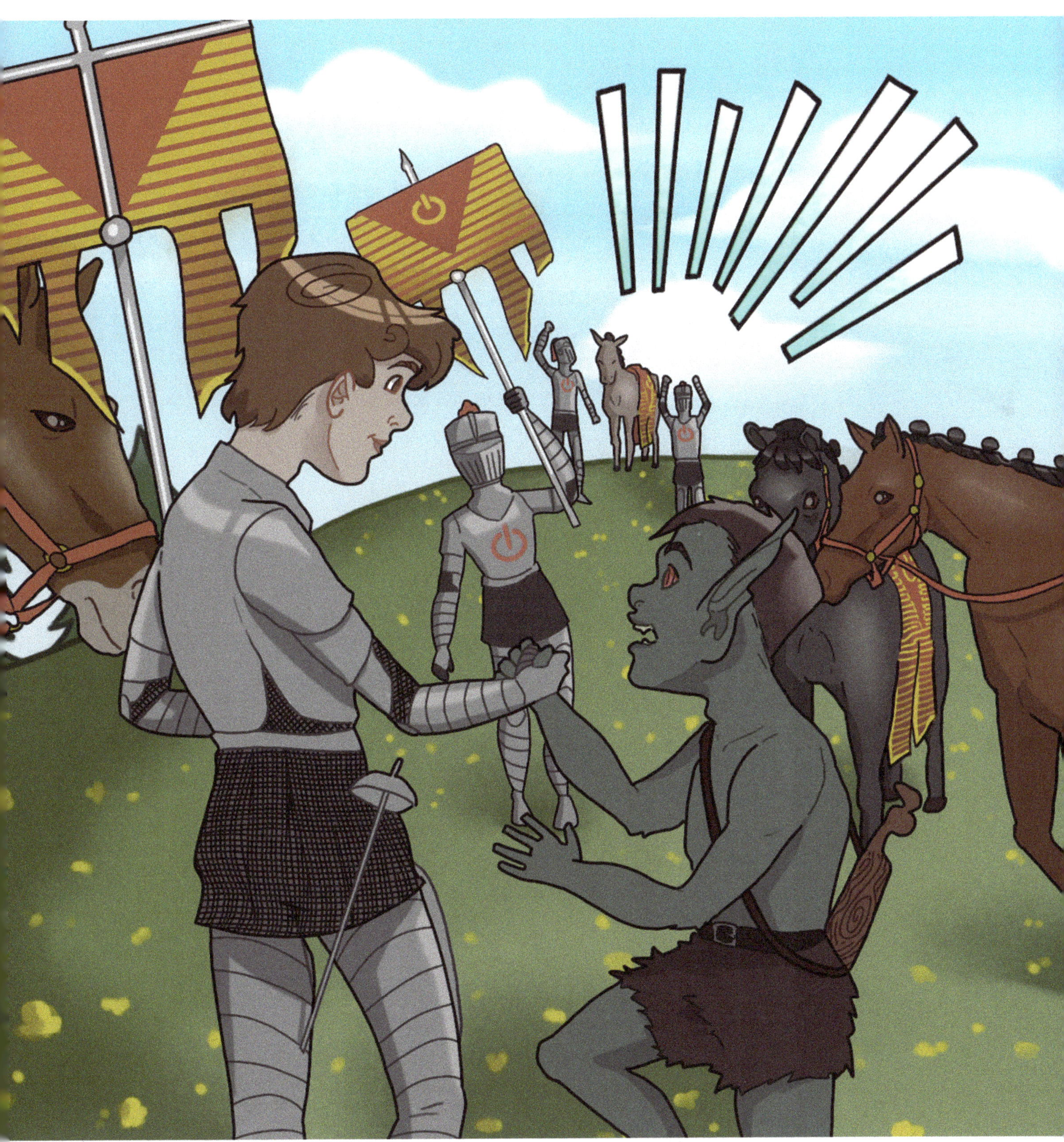

For a long time Lewis the Troll seemed to want to help all the knights and Breck on their quests.

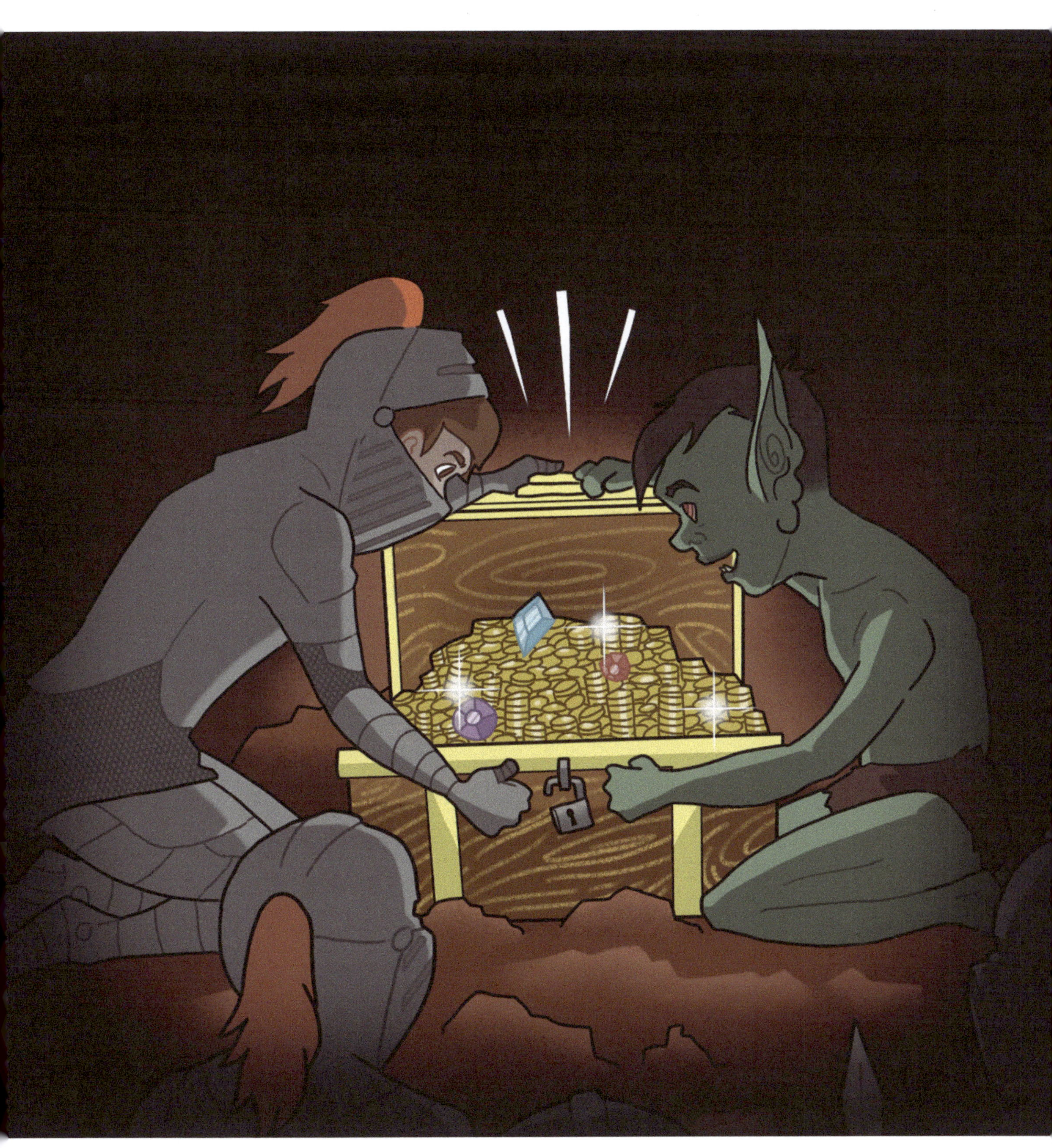

Lewis the Troll said that he lived in a faraway kingdom, in a castle with lots of money, and the best knight equipment in the world.

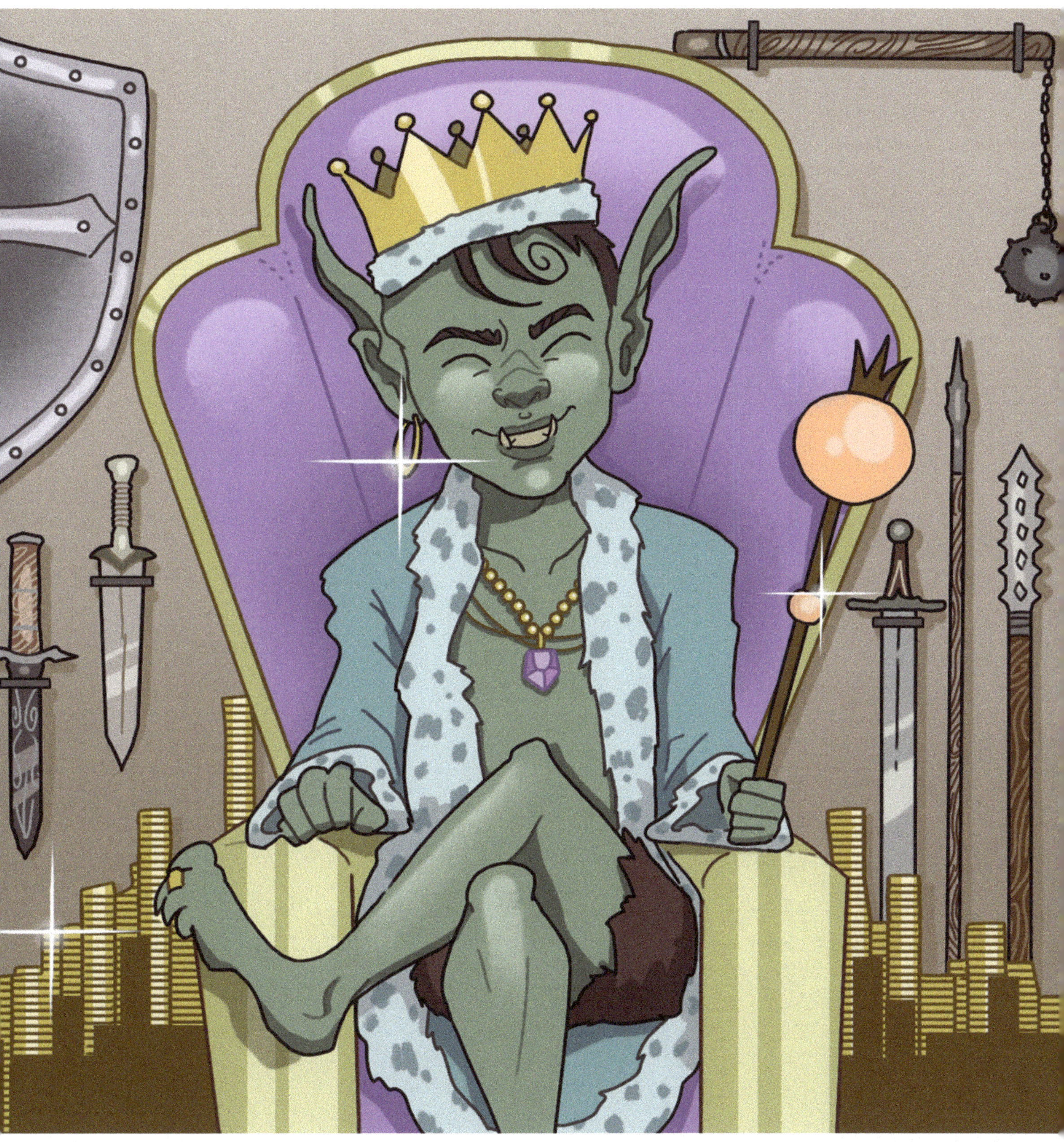

Breck's knight friends started not to believe what Lewis the Troll said.

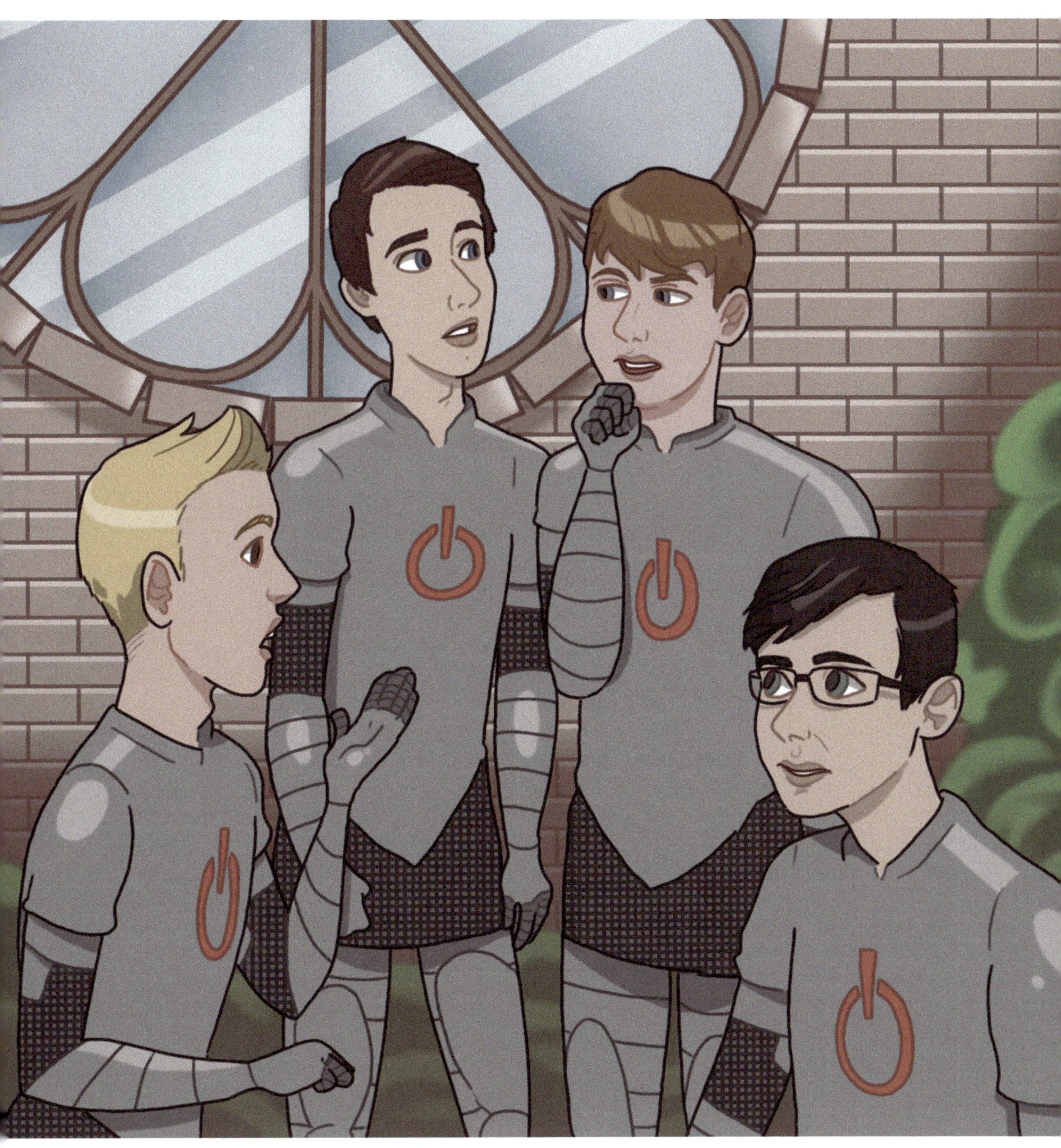

Lewis the Troll seemed to have a special interest in Breck and spent lots of time telling Breck that if he came with him to his kingdom all his dreams would come true.

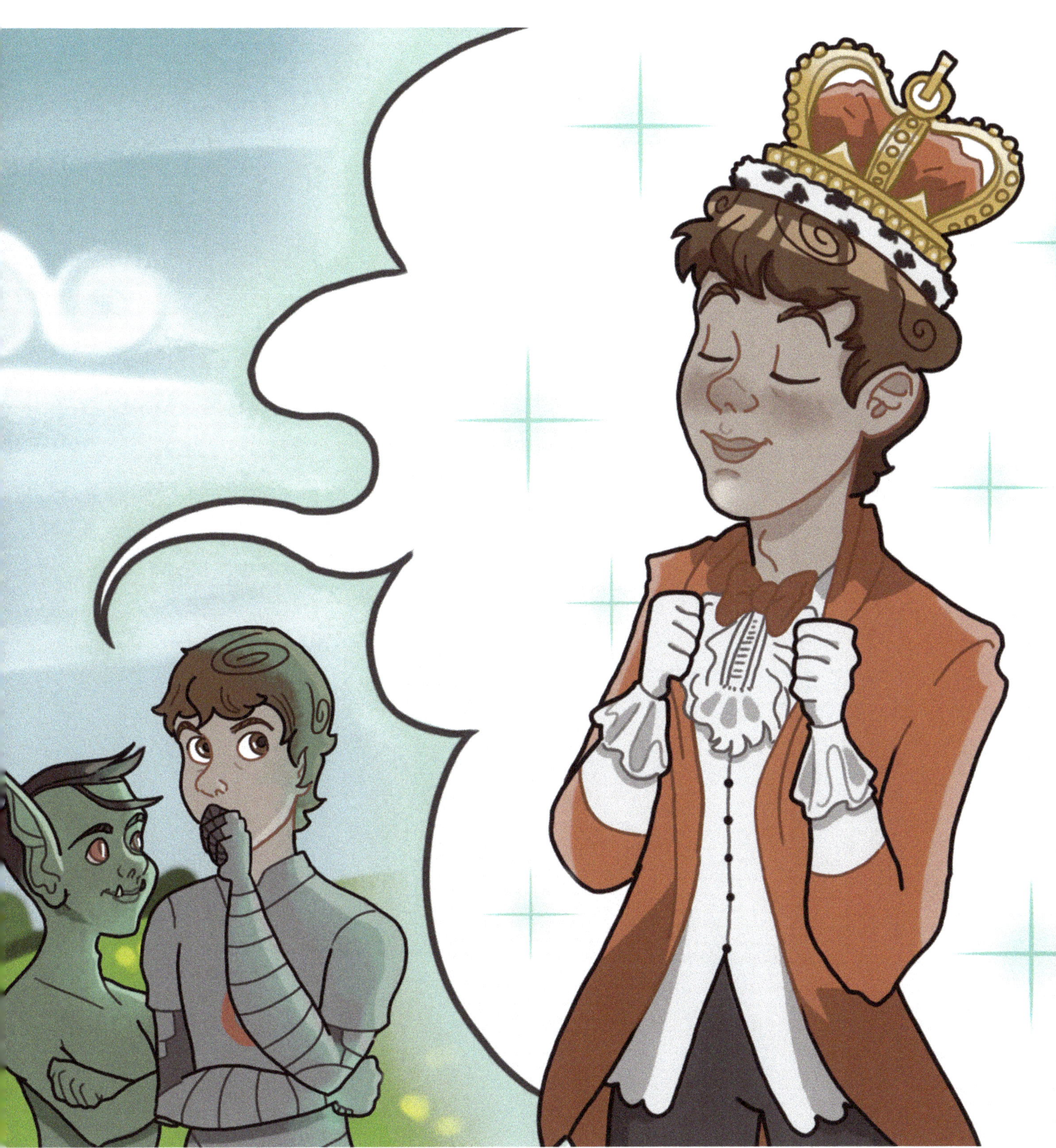

One day, Lewis the Troll wrote a letter to Breck. The letter said "If you come to my kingdom you will get to rule as King. But you must not tell anyone, including your mum, the Queen."

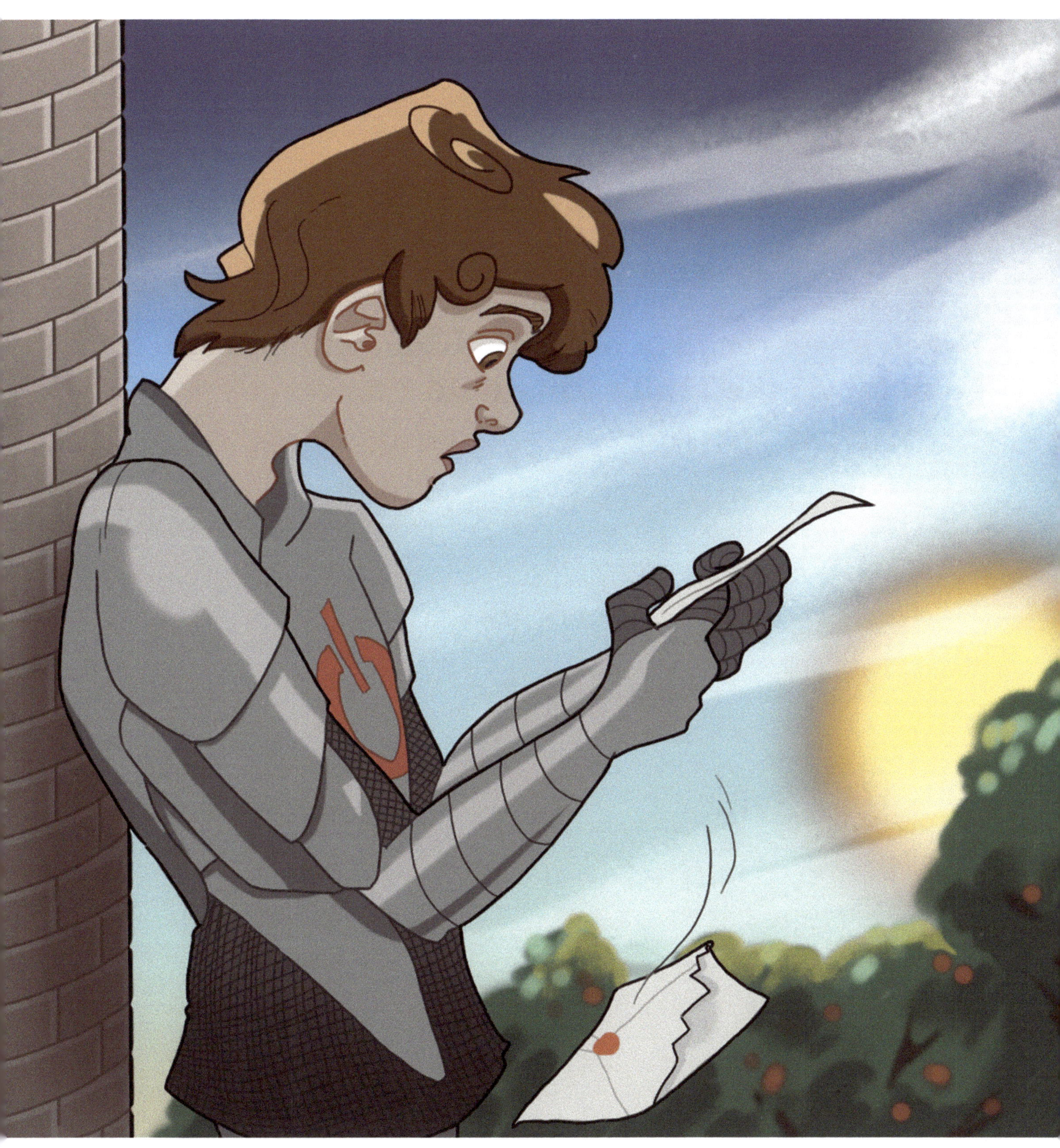

Breck loved the idea of being King. So he decided to go to Lewis the Troll's kingdom.

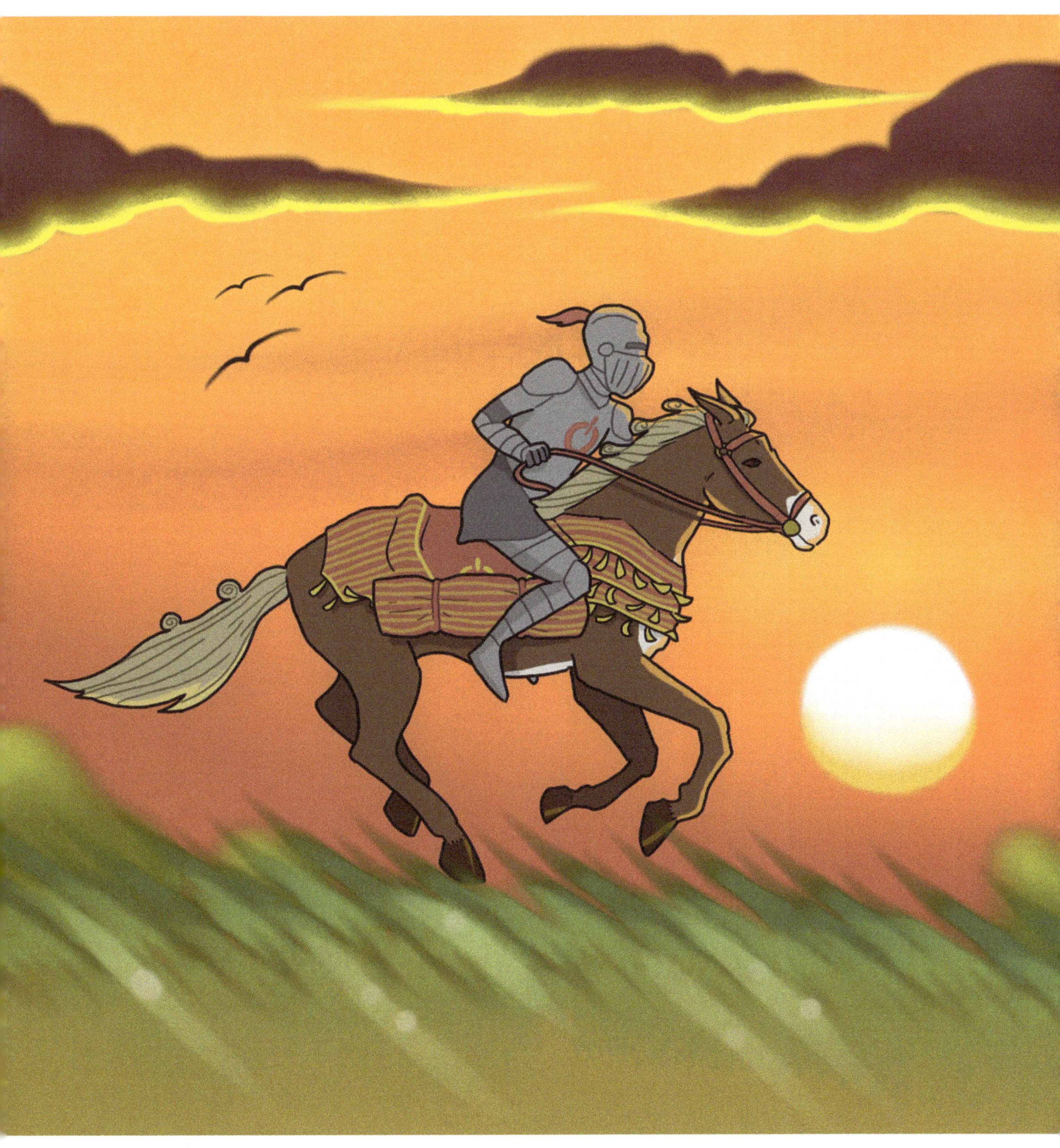

When Breck arrived at Lewis the Troll's kingdom, none of what Lewis had said was true. But he was a long way from home and...

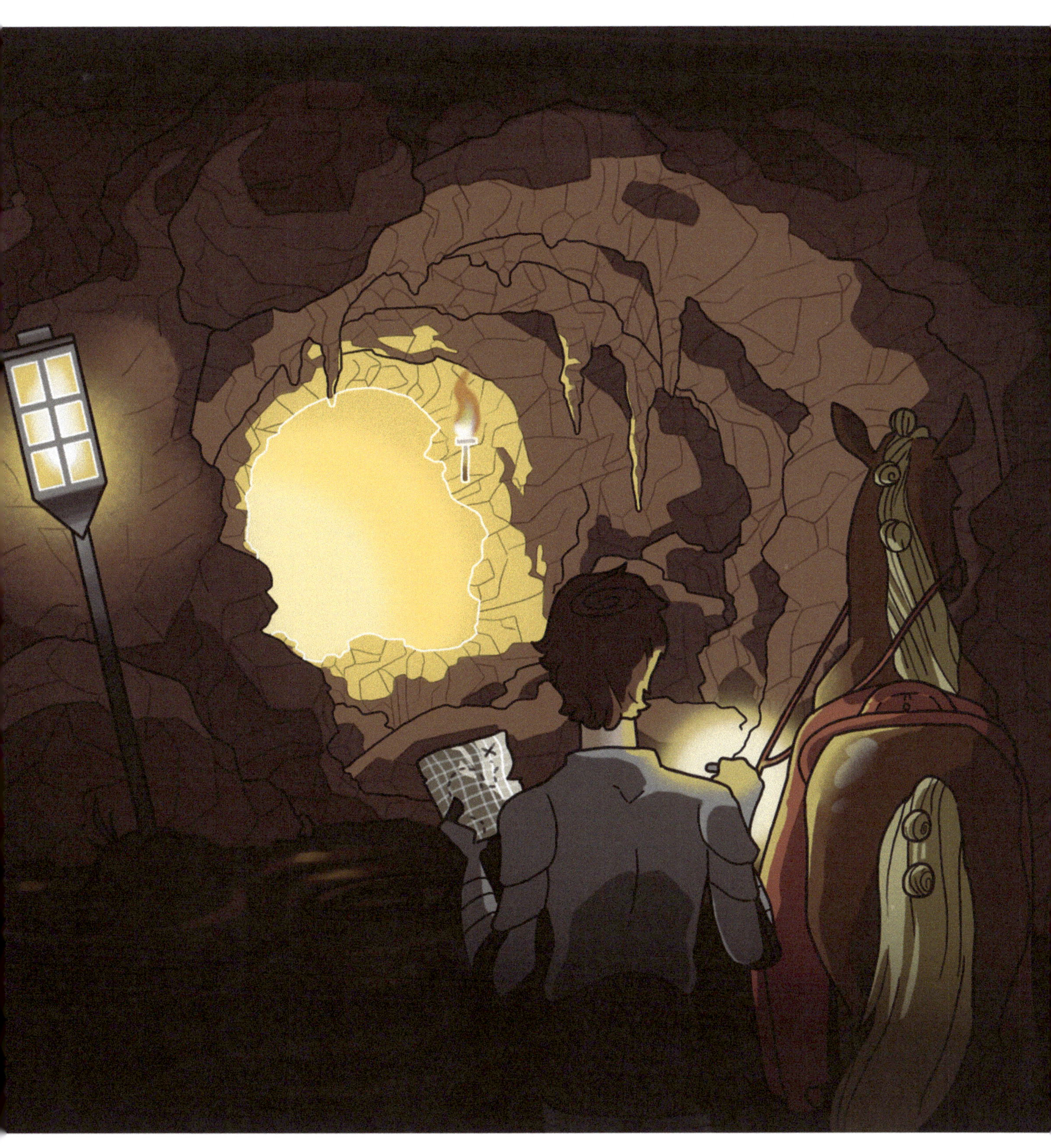

There was no happy ending.

This is not a fairy tale.

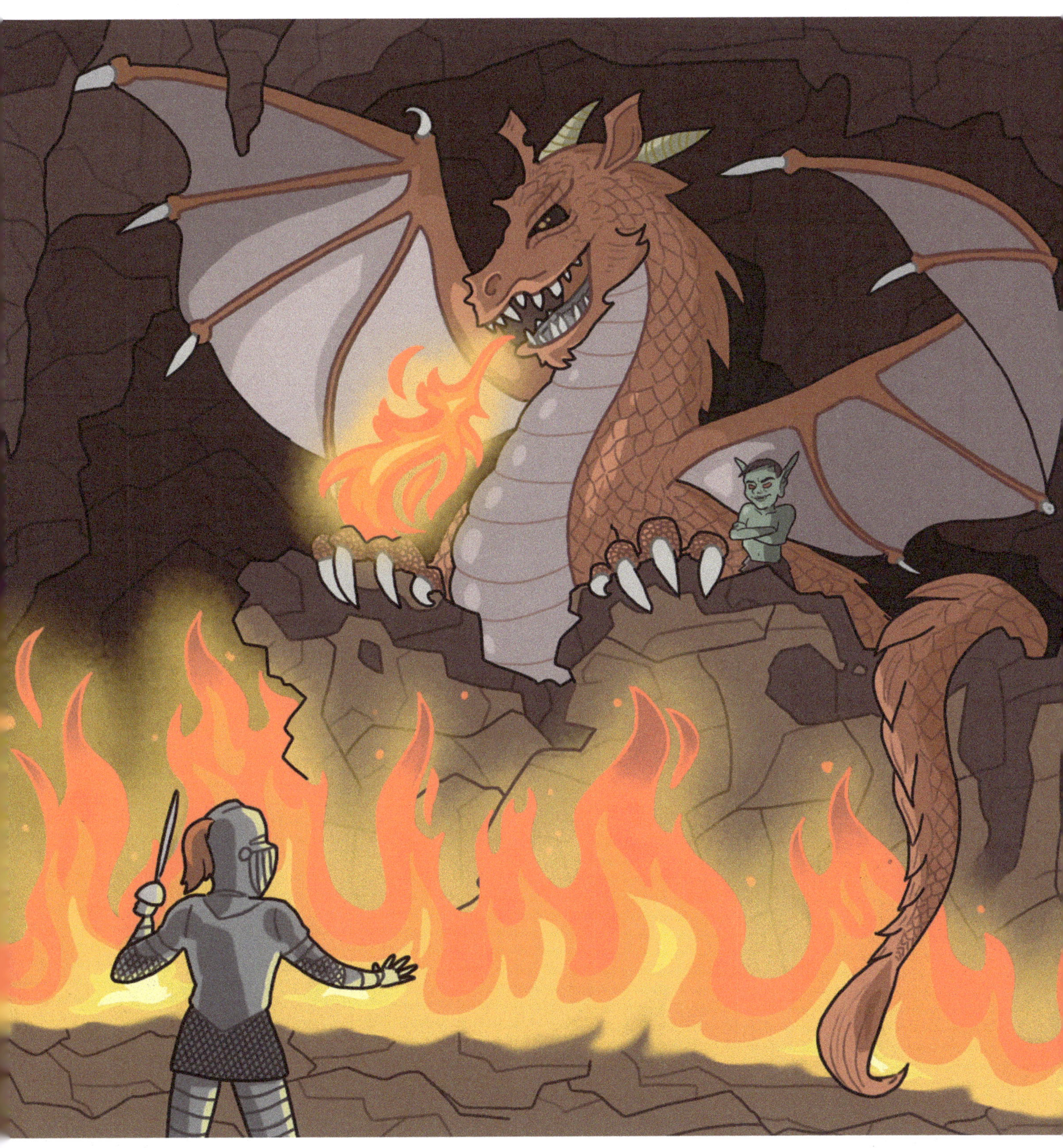

This is a true story.

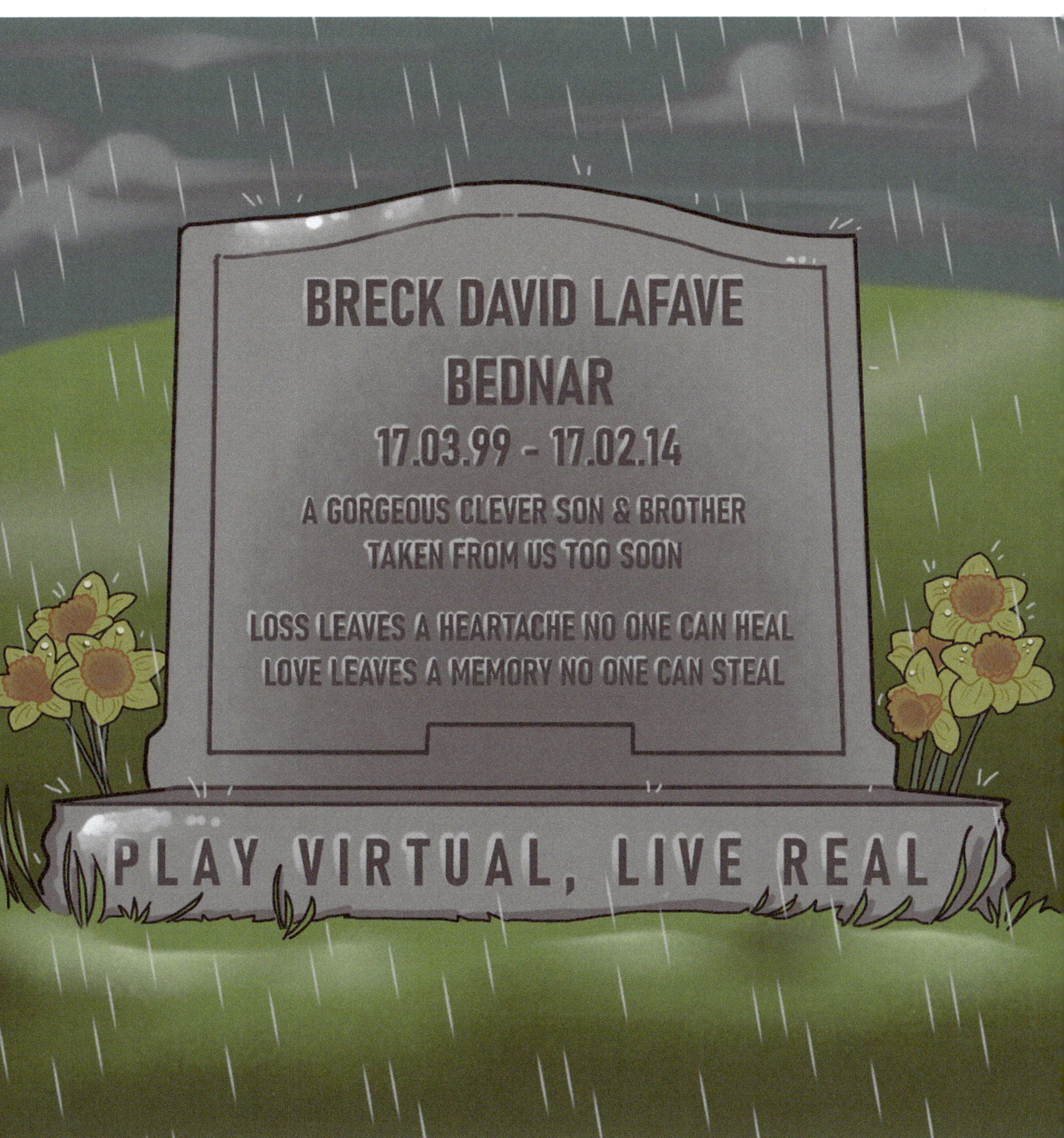
BRECK DAVID LAFAVE
BEDNAR
17.03.99 - 17.02.14
A GORGEOUS CLEVER SON & BROTHER
TAKEN FROM US TOO SOON
LOSS LEAVES A HEARTACHE NO ONE CAN HEAL
LOVE LEAVES A MEMORY NO ONE CAN STEAL
PLAY VIRTUAL, LIVE REAL

There was a 14-year-old boy named Breck.

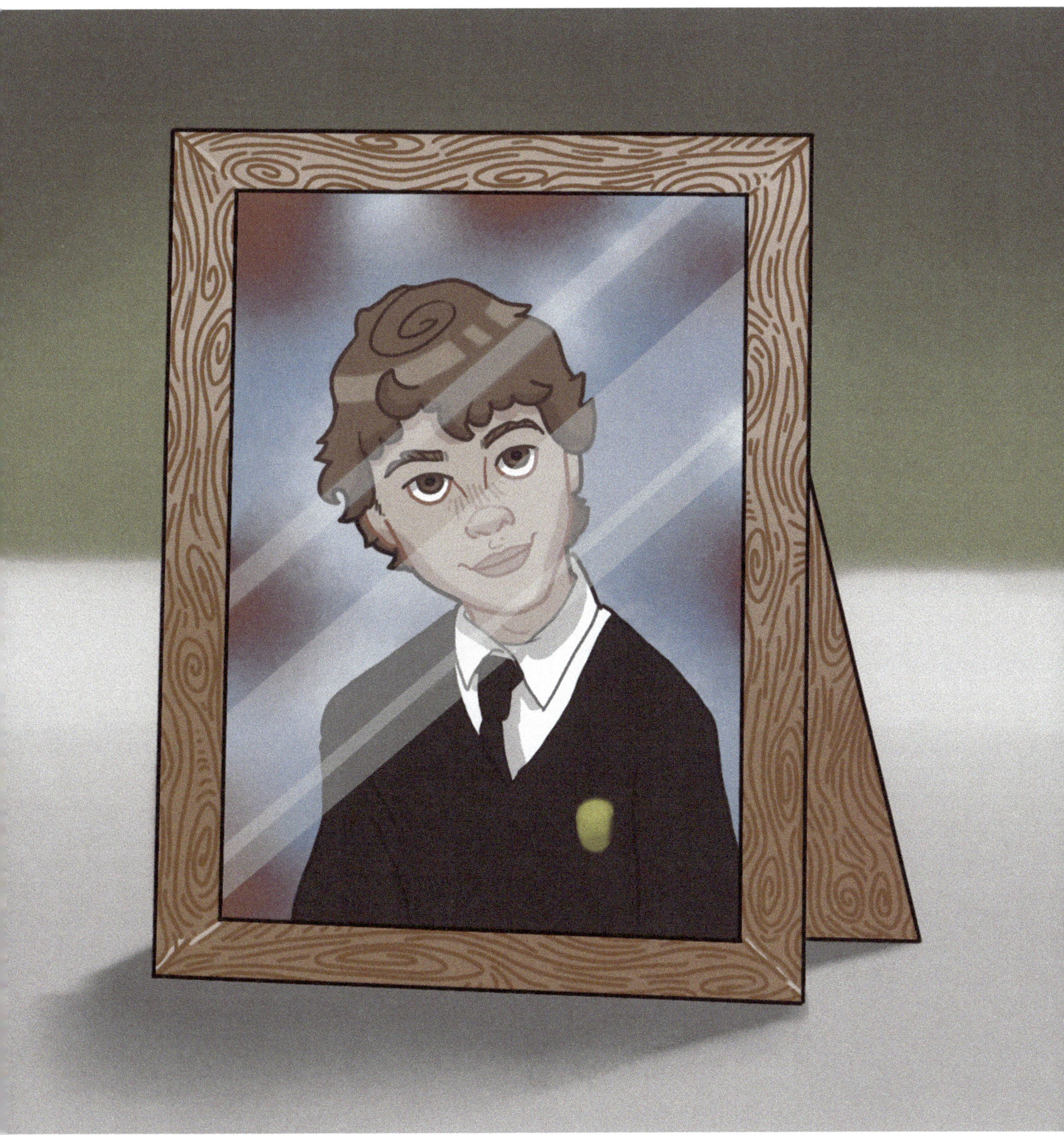

Breck enjoyed gaming with his friends on the computer online.

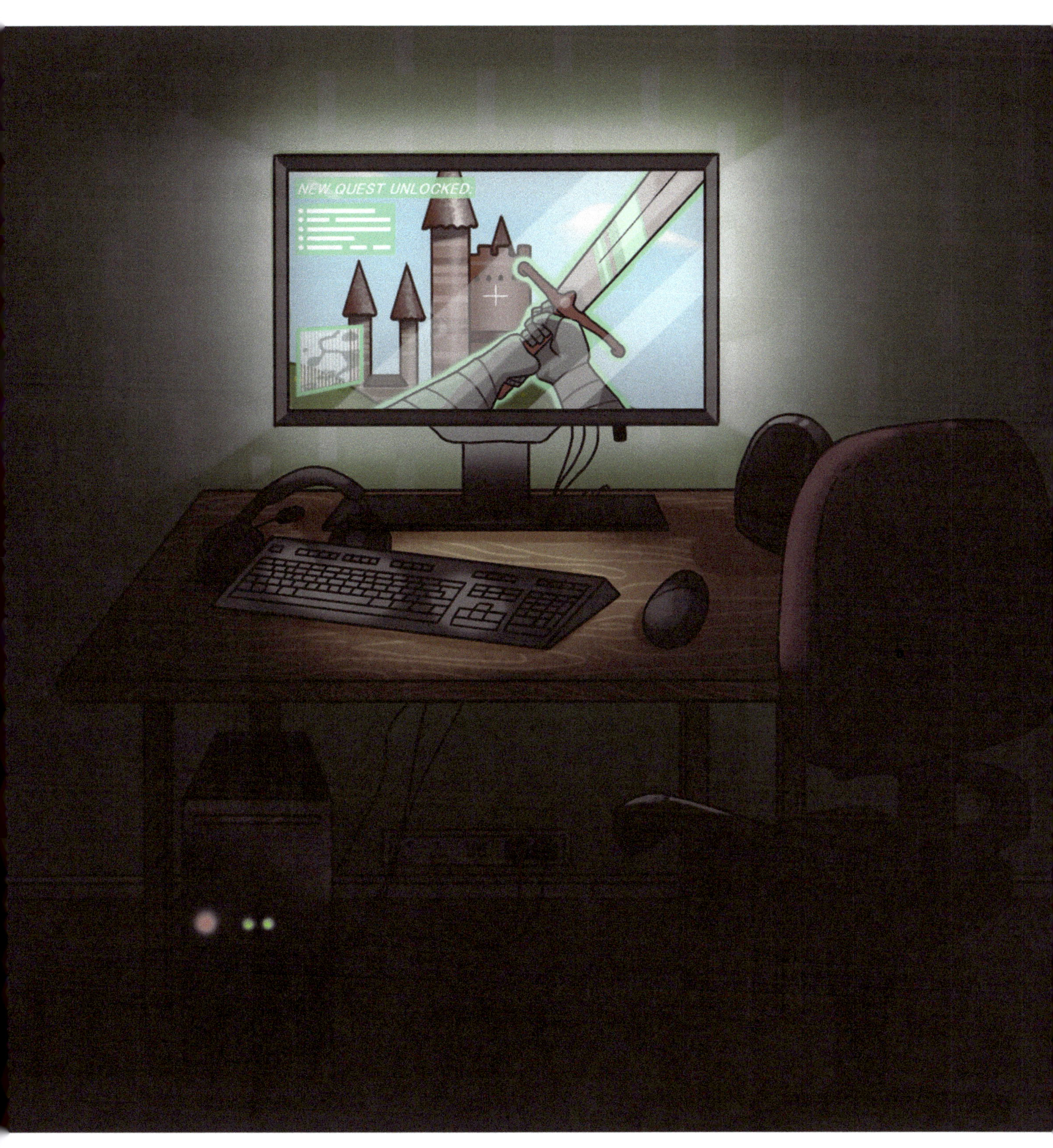
NEW QUEST UNLOCKED.

One day an 18-year-old man called Lewis asked to join Breck's friends on their computer games.

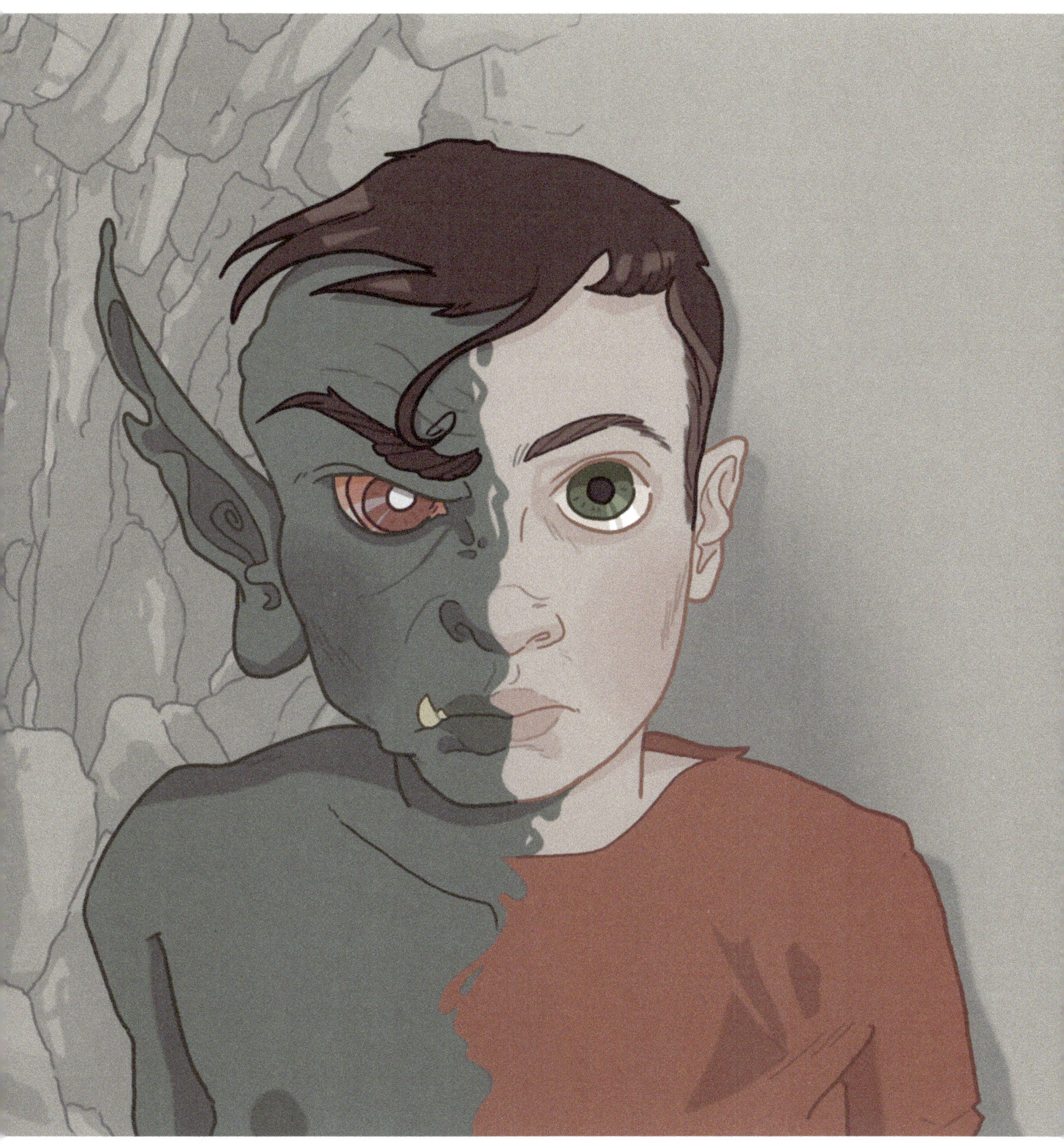

Lewis said to Breck and his friends that he had lots of money, had a gaming business, and mansions.

Breck's friends started not to believe Lewis. Breck's Mum didn't believe Lewis either.

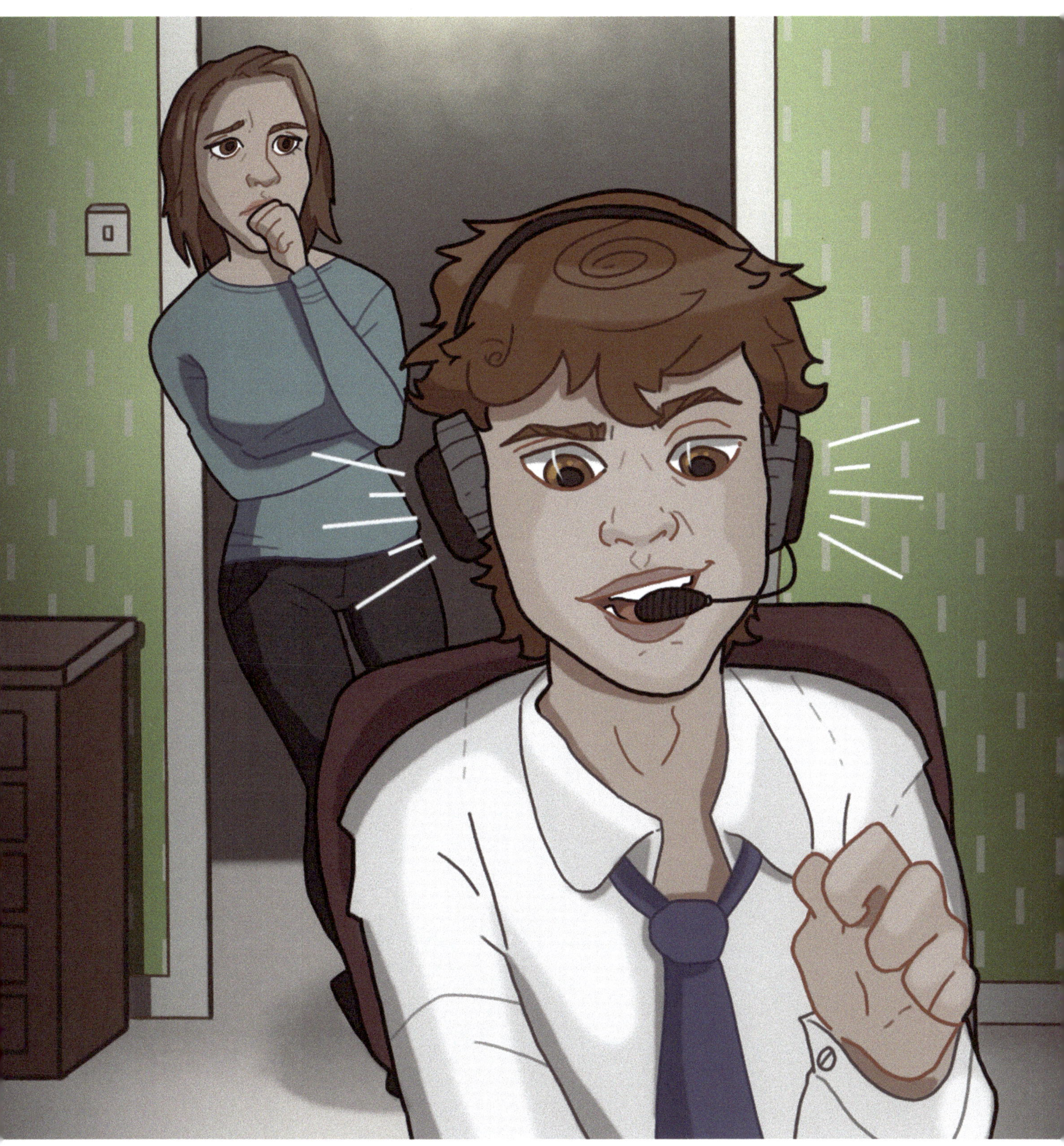

Lewis pushed Breck away from his friends and family with his lies.

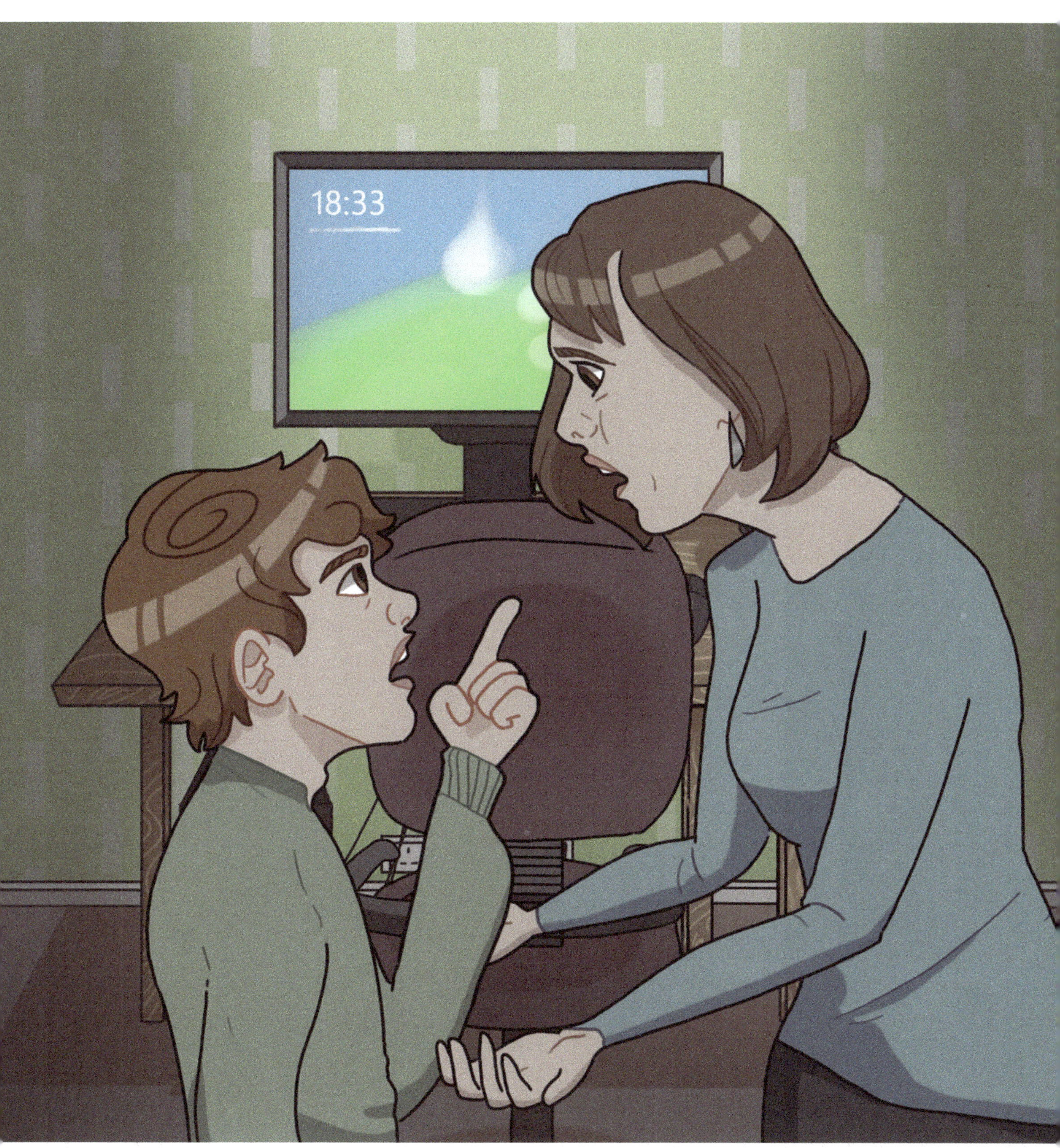
18:33

Lewis lied that he was ill and going to die. Lewis said that if Breck came to his house all Lewis's money, business, and houses would belong to Breck. However, he said he must not tell his Mum that they were meeting.

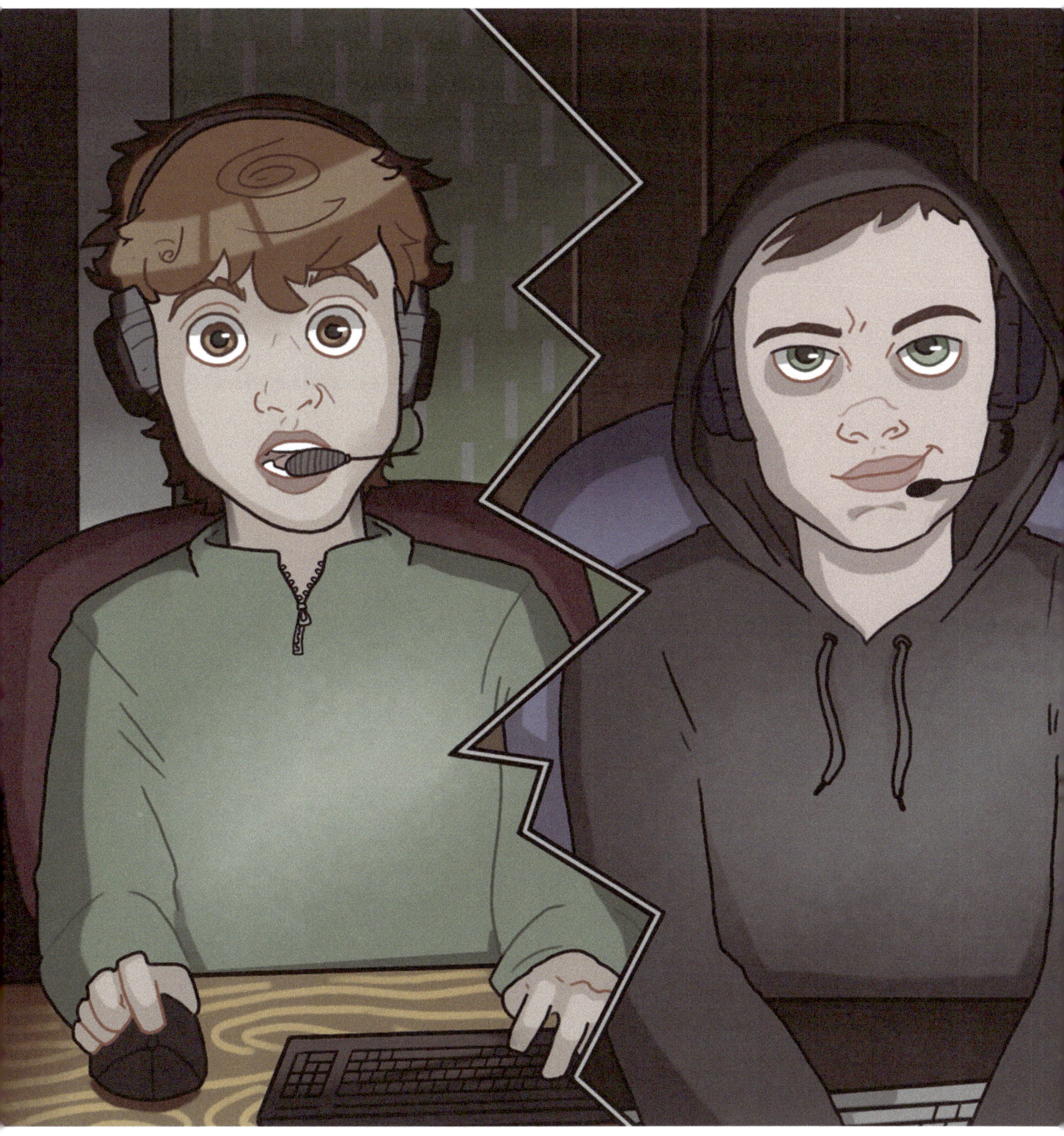

Breck lied to his friends and family and went to Lewis's home without telling anyone where he was going.

Breck ended up an hour from home.

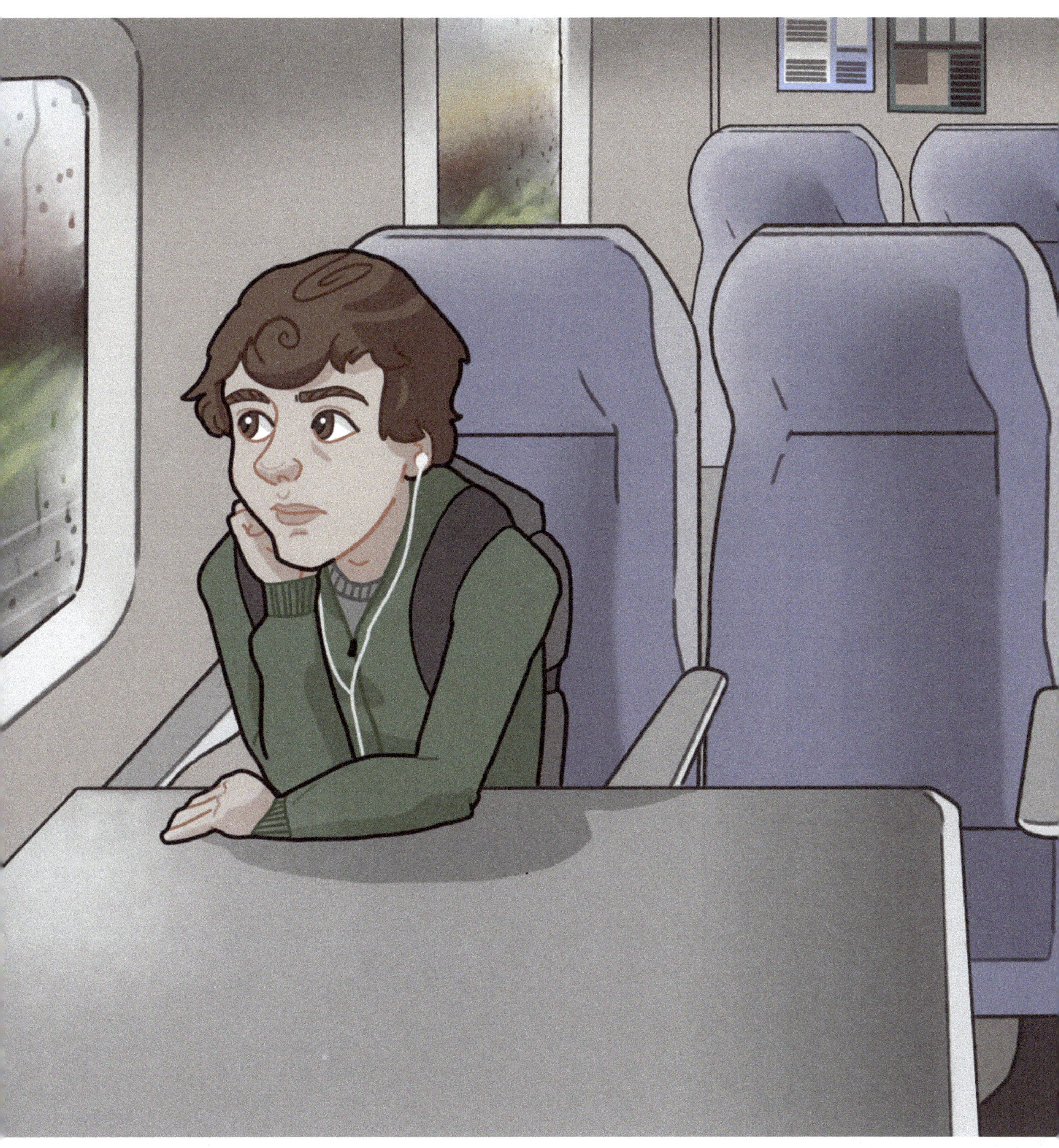

Lewis lived in a small flat.

Lewis did not have riches.

Lewis did not have a business for Breck.

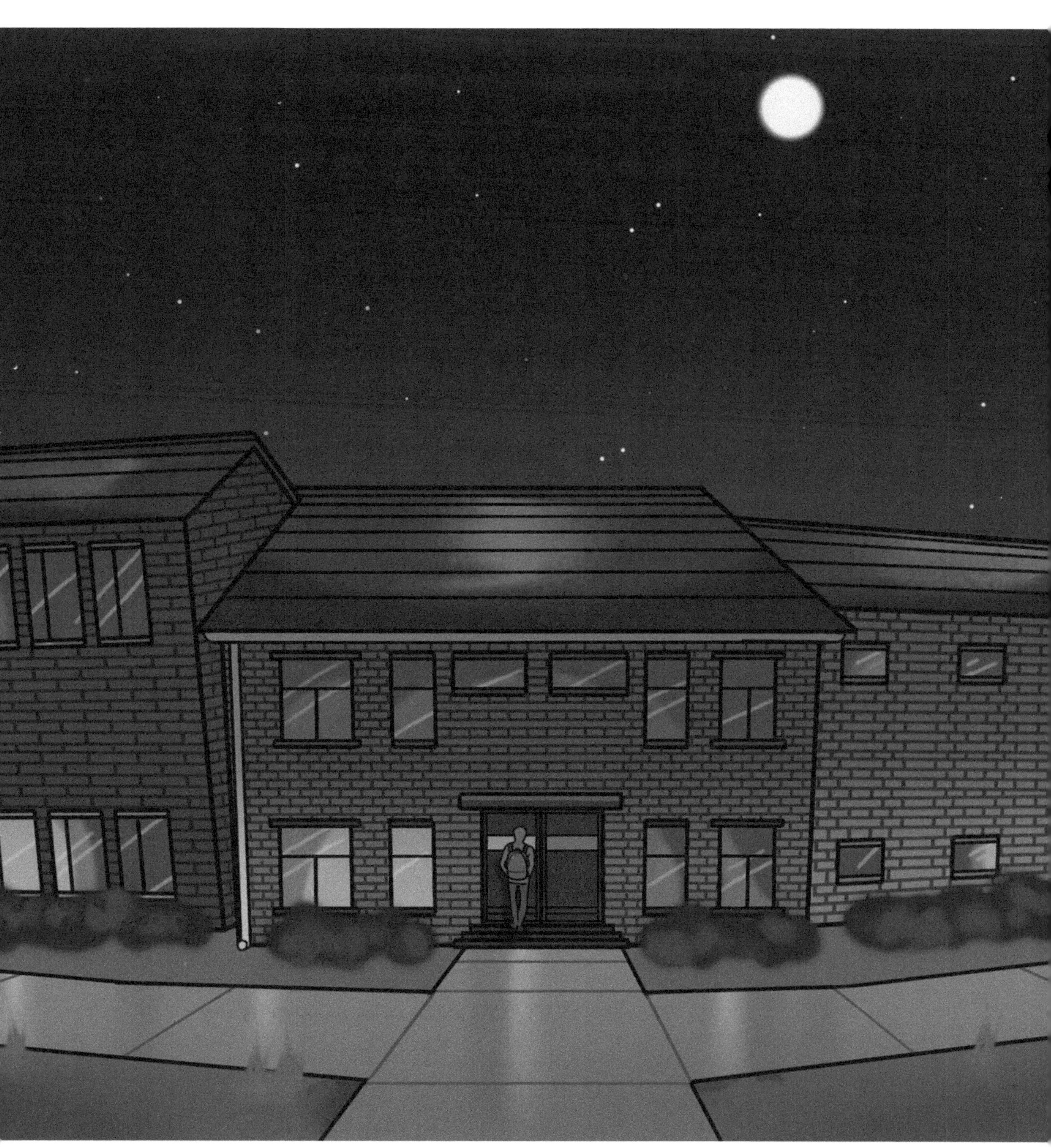

Lewis wanted to hurt Breck.

Breck went in alive…

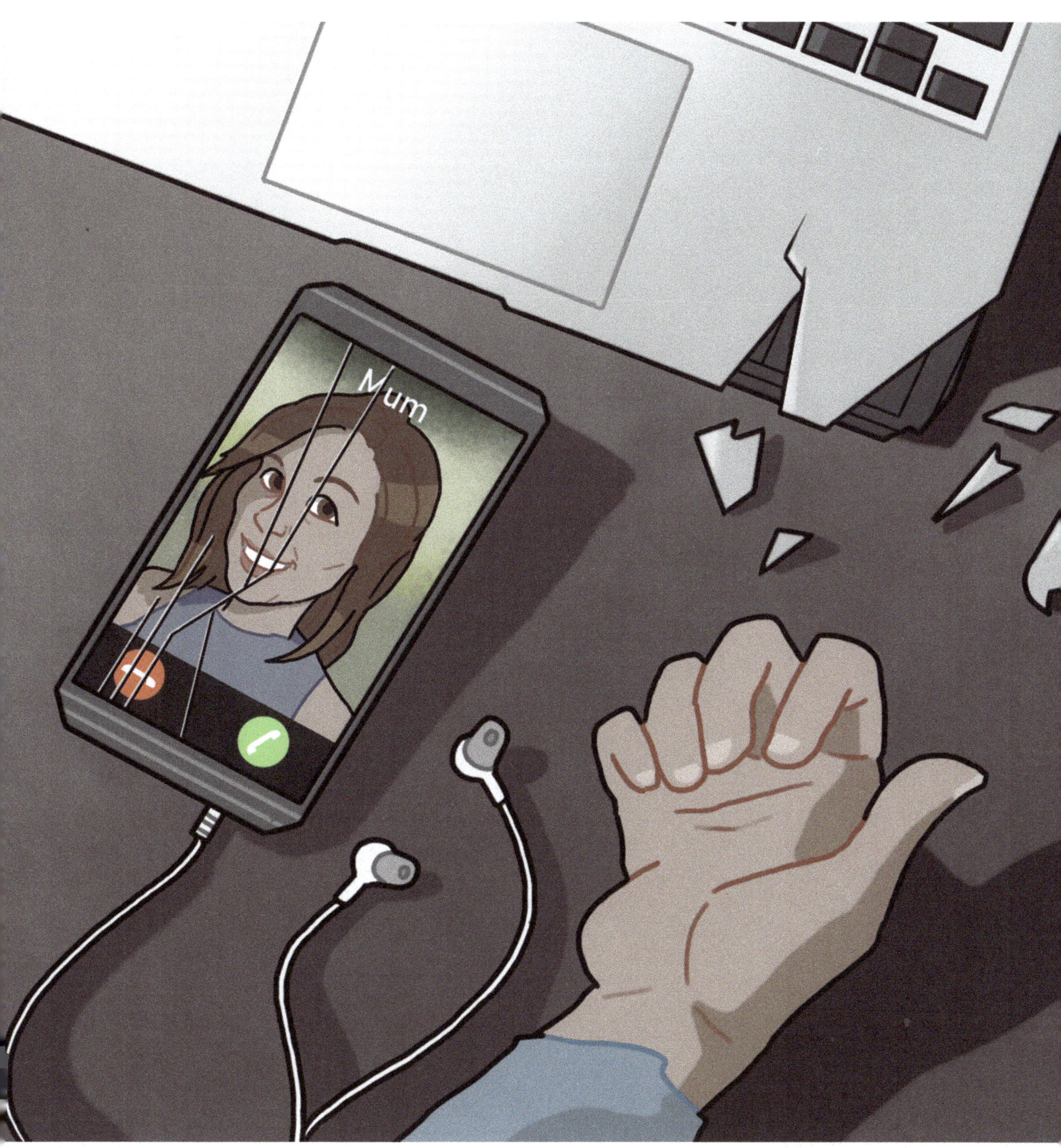
Mum

Breck came out dead.

Lewis killed Breck.

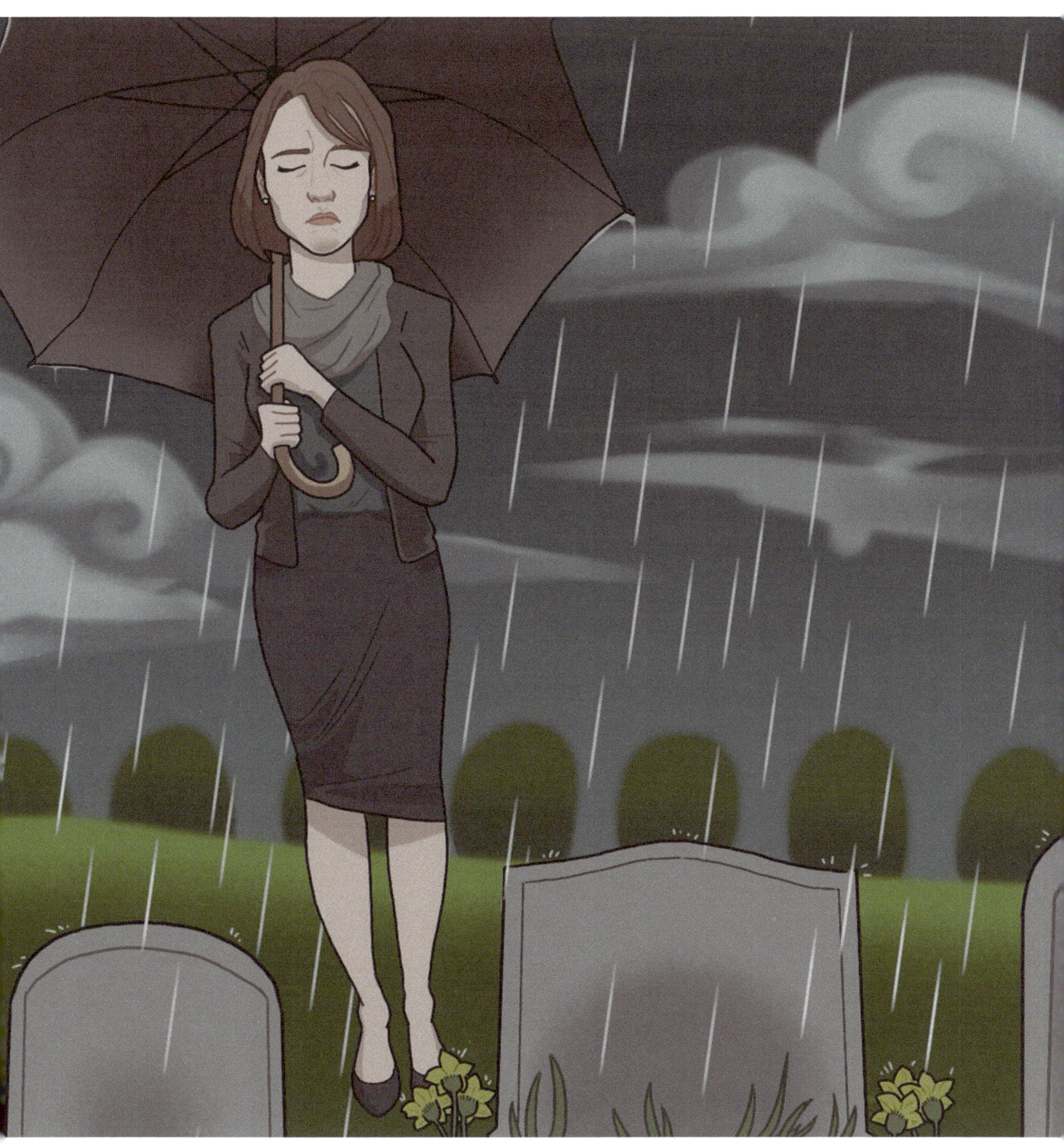

Remember Breck.

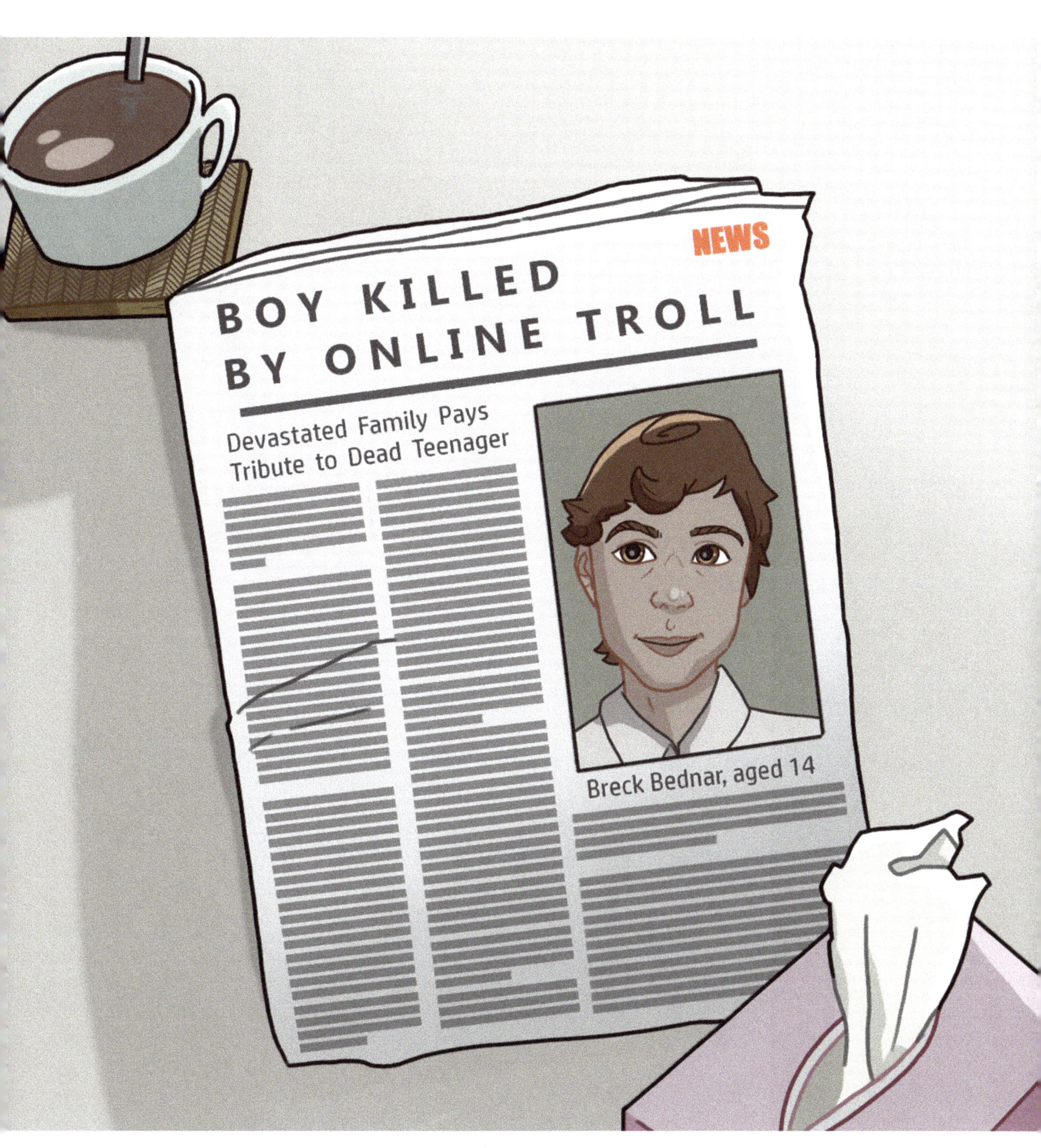
NEWS
BOY KILLED BY ONLINE TROLL
Devastated Family Pays Tribute to Dead Teenager
Breck Bednar, aged 14

The Breck Principles

The Breck Foundation is raising awareness for playing safe whilst using the internet.
Keep safe by following these simple principles that we have created using Breck's name.

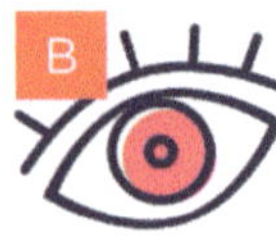

Be aware & believe

Be aware of the real and increasing dangers today's children may face online.
Believe that there are people who use the internet to groom, abuse and exploit young people.

Report it

Report any concerns immediately to school, police, Childline, NSPCC or CEOP.
Even small pieces of information when put together can make up the bigger picture of what may be happening to a child online.

Educate & Empower

Educate others on the signs of grooming and exploitation.
Be empowered to act on concerns.

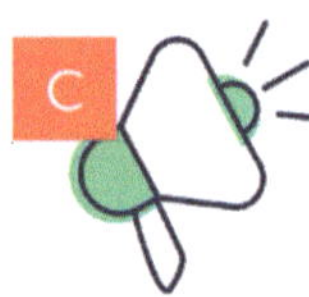

Communicate

Encourage and support young people to communicate concerns about themselves or how their peers are behaving online. Support others by sharing these principles within your community.

Know the signs & Keep safe

Know the signs of grooming and exploitation.
Keeping safe online must be everyone's priority!

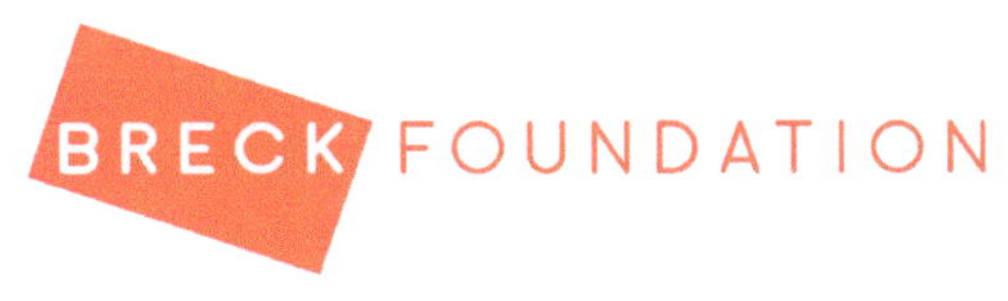

Scheme of Work

SUBJECT: PHSE/English/Drama/ICT/Assembly or Class Presentation

TOPIC/UNIT: Breck and the Online Troll: Online Grooming and Keeping Safe

NO. OF LESSONS: Six

About the unit:

'Breck and the Online Troll' is aimed at learners with a cognitive age of 8-11 years old.

The aim of this scheme of work is to introduce the story of Breck Bednar and begin instilling an understanding of online safety and online grooming.

Students will study:

- The story of Breck Bednar
- Dealing with truth and lies
- Good and bad things about the internet
- Who to talk to about online worries
- What is grooming?
- Feelings involved in grooming
- Presenting and sharing the message of the Breck Foundation

Resources can be used to support and consolidate learning. Please change story writing wherever needed to a size, font or symbol that best supports your students.

The book can be used as a tool to prepare for an assembly or or to share internet safety information with another class. As you go through the story, give students roles and lines within the text. Equally, you can develop your own lines and characters to complement what you are presenting.

If, during the process of studying this text, a student asks to speak to staff or divulges any safeguarding concerns, please follow your facility's safeguarding procedures.

The Breck foundation is continually developing resources. We are currently developing music that will be available to support students with emotional literacy enabling communication of the story. These pieces of music could be used during or at the end of your storytelling or presentations. They could be sung and signed by the groups.

Please share any work you create with the Breck Foundation on social media using @breckfoundation.

For further information and resources please go to **www.breckfoundation.org**.

Warning to educators:

Students will be introduced to a simple outline of the events surrounding the death of Breck Bednar.

Please inform parents and guardians that their child will be studying online safety with a focus on the Breck Bednar story. This is important due to the wide range of videos and interviews that are available online and across social media. If you feel it is appropriate, you may want to arrange a meeting with parents to discuss how they can support their children's learning during this scheme of work. Please see Appendix 1 for an example of a guide letter to parents and guardians.

Learning intentions	Teaching activities	Differentiation/Points to note	Resources
To understand the story of 'Breck and the Online Troll'. To understand that Breck was a real person To understand what was real and fake in the 'Breck and Online Troll' story	• Introduce the idea that you are going to be studying the book 'Breck and the Online Troll'. • Ask if anyone knows anything about Breck. • Study the cover of the book - what could the story be about? • Read 'Breck and the Online Troll'. • Give time for the story to sink in. Offer some time of reflection. You could put a piece of music on. • Read the story again and ask the group what they think is fake about the story and what is real. Explain that this is a true story and this really did happen. • Explain that we are learning this story to keep ourselves and others safe on the internet. • Give each student a piece of paper that says Fake or True. • Explain to the students that some of what we hear and read on the internet is fake news. Give students an example such as 'Pigs have started to grow wings', to test the waters and see how students respond. • Then use situations for the story to prompt responses; e.g. Breck was a real person, Lewis had lots of money, Breck's mum didn't know what was going on. • Use Appendix 3: Fake News and True Story and Appendix 4: Sentences for Fake News and True Story. • Students can cut out the sentences and stick them onto the chart to show whether they think the sentences are fake or real about the story. • When the students have completed this, go through the work and see if there are any conflicting answers. • At the end of the lesson reiterate to students that Breck was a real person and these horrible things did happen to him. However, these situations are rare and we are trying to help protect our students, not scare them.	1. Please adapt the writing in the books to the size or symbol that is suitable for your class group 2. Some students may need to stop the lesson and have some further time to process. Please give this extra time and space. 3. Choose wording of computer/ internet carefully. Students may think that groomers only work through the internet if you use the phrase internet. Try using computer and internet together. 4. When doing the fake news and real story within the book, you may want to have Fake one side of the room and True the other side of the room. You could get the students to go to the area in the room if they think its fake or true. 5. When using Appendix 3, you may want students to write the ideas down rather than cut them out.	1. 'Breck and the Online Troll' student and teacher editions 2. Appendix 2: Picture of Breck 3. Pieces of paper with Fake on one side and True on the other 4. Appendix 3: Fake News and True story 5. Appendix 4: Sentences for Fake News and true Story 6. Scissors 7. Glue 8. Pens (optional) BRECK FOUNDATION

Learning intentions	Teaching activities	Differentiation/Points to note	Resources
	• Finally remind students not to believe everything they hear or see on the internet/gaming especially if it is from someone they don't even know.		
To recall the story of 'Breck and the Online Troll'. To identify people that can be trusted	• Re-introduce the story of 'Breck and the Online Troll'. • To do this, play the fool and say you have forgotten the words to the story. See if students one at a time can recall what is going on in the images. • Introduce the idea that you want the students to share their work with another class or the school. Ask students to take on the roles of each character and act out as you read the story. • Give students time to process the story again. Use a short music track or reflection time. • Explain to students that the end of the story could have been very different, if more people had spoken out. Breck's friends all knew Lewis but none of them told their parents they were worried. • Explain to students that there are adults that we can trust and should tell them things if we are worried or scared about something. • See if any students can come up with a list of trusted people. Use some examples of people that students should not speak to consolidate learning, ie the lady you sit next to on the public bus • Use Appendix 5: People that I can speak to when worried and Appendix 6: List of People for students to select to whom they think they should talk when they are worried. Students can cut out the names and stick them onto the sheet. • After the worksheet is complete, get students to share who their trusted adults are. • Assure students that if they are worried or scared or anything it is important to share with any of the trusted adults they have listed.	• Please adapt the writing in the books to the size or symbol that is suitable to your class group. • When telling the story you may want to begin using props to tell the story. • When introducing the idea of people that the students can trust you may want to use pictures of different people include images of the students' parents or guardians where possible. • When working on the worksheet Appendix 4, change to symbols where needed or get students to write out their answers. Students can also use names of people. Some students may prefer to use photographs of the people that they trust.	• 'Breck and the Online Troll' Student or Teacher edition • Appendix 5: People I can speak to when I am worried. • Appendix 6: List of people • Glue • Scissors • Pen (optional) BRECK FOUNDATION

Learning intentions	Teaching activities	Differentiation/Points to note	Resources
To recall the story of 'Breck and the Online Troll' To recall who are trusted people are To understand the good and bad issues of the internet and computing	• Begin by asking the students who one of their trusted people is. • Remind students that we should share our worries and fears about computing and the internet with everyone. • Ask one student to take the lead on teaching the story to see if they can get it right. • Remind students that they are going to share what they have learnt with other students in the school • Select students who are going to play each role. • Re-read the story 'Breck and the Online Troll'. Ask the students if they would like time out between. • If you feel the students need it, give them reflection time. • When you come back together as a group get a large piece of paper. On one side write 'good' and on the other 'bad'. • Ask students to think of what good things computers and the internet are for. Write down any ideas shared. • Then turn the paper over, what bad things can the internet and computing be used for. Get students to think about Breck's story and the bad things that happened to him. • Students can then use Appendix 7 and 8 to consolidate their learning. Students can cut and stick the words where they feel is appropriate. • At the end of the lesson, reassure students that computers and the internet are great tools. Few people in the world use them to hurt other people. Remind students that if there is something that is upsetting someone they should speak to a trusted adult.	• Please adapt the writing in the books to the size or symbol that is suitable to your class group. • When using Appendix 7, students can write on the sheet rather than stick.	• 'Breck and the Online Troll' Student or Teacher edition • Large piece of paper • Board marker • Appendix 7: Good and bad things about computing and the internet • Appendix 8: Words for good and bad things about computing and the internet. • Glue • Scissors • Pen (optional) BRECK FOUNDATION

Learning intentions	Teaching activities	Differentiation/Points to note	Resources
To understand the story of 'Breck and the Online Troll'. To develop presentation skills To understand about grooming	• Begin with reminding students that you are presenting the story to other students/classes. • Remind students that they are educating others too. • Rehearse your presentation by telling the story and students acting out. • You may want to rehearse/practice this two or three times. • If students need reflection time after this, offer it to them with music or quiet time. • When the group comes together ask the question, 'What is grooming?' • Give students time to respond. • Explain to students that grooming is where someone abuses someone's trust and makes them do things that they would not normally do. • Explain to the students that Lewis groomed Breck. Lewis lied to him to gain his trust; he changed Breck to the point where he was lying to his family. Was Lewis rich, famous, have a nice, car, job or home? No, he only wanted to hurt Breck. • Get a series of photos of people of different sex, age and race. Ask the students to choose who they think could be a groomer from the pictures. • Explain that any of the people could be groomers. Anyone who tries to manipulate you or make you do something you feel is wrong, could be a groomer. • In small groups, use Appendix 9: What is grooming? And Appendix 10: Grooming sentence ideas. Each person should read one of the sentences and decide whether that is a groomer or not. Some of the answers may require some further discussion. Students can cut out the sentences and stick onto the sheet. • At the end of the lesson, discuss with students their answers. Were any of them harder to make a decision about?	• Please adapt the writing in the books to the size or symbol that is suitable to your class group. • When selecting images you may want to use the image of Lewis that was released by the police. • When using Appendix 9 Students may just want to write on their sheets or cut and stick.	• 'Breck and the Online Troll' Student or Teacher edition • Photos of different people • Appendix 9: What is grooming? And Appendix 10: Grooming sentence ideas • Scissors • Glue BRECK FOUNDATION

Learning intentions	Teaching activities	Differentiation/Points to note	Resources
	• At the end of the lesson, remind students that not everyone who tries to help and care for us is a groomer. Most people want what is best for us. • Remind students that if they feel they are being made to do something they don't like or feel they are being hurt by someone they must tell an adult. Equally if they are worried about a friend or family member they must tell a trusted adult.		
To create a play from the story of 'Breck and the Online Troll'. To develop emotional understanding	• Begin by reminding students they are going to share what they have learnt with someone (a class or the rest of school) in the next week. • Pretend that you have forgotten what happens in your students' play. Ask the students to present the play to you. • Give students feedback on how you think their play went. • Get students to rehearse again with your feedback. • If needed give children time to reflect; this can be to music. • When you come back in a group, ask them to make a list of feelings, as many as they can. • Ask students how they feel right now and get them to feedback. • Get the students to split into three groups. Give each group a person, Lorin (Breck's Mum), Lewis and Breck. • Rotate every three minutes asking the students how this person may feel about what happened to them during the story. • Share the ideas with the group. • Students can then individually use Appendix 11: How do they feel and Appendix 12: Feelings. Students can cut out and stick on the different feelings that each person may have during the story. • Ask students to leave the one about themselves to last. • With the last one, ask students to write down how they feel when they hear the story about Breck.	• Please adapt the writing in the books to the size or symbol that is suitable to your class group • When working in groups on how each person might feel, it might be better for your class to work as a whole rather than separate groups. • Students may want to write their own answers on the work sheet.	• Any props you are using to support the storytelling • Large piece of paper • Board marker • Appendix 11: How do they feel • Appendix 12: How do they feel sentences • Glue • Scissors • Pen (optional)

Learning intentions	Teaching activities	Differentiation/Points to note	Resources
	• At the end of the lesson, discuss with the students that it is good to talk about our feelings and that it is good to share how we feel. Remind students if they have worries or fears they should discuss with a trusted adult.		
To teach others the story of 'Breck and the Online Troll' To consolidate learning To share the Breck Foundation message	• At this point students should have presented their work to someone, a class or the school. • Firstly, congratulate students on doing a good job. • Share videos or images from their presentation with students. • Using Appendix 13: Storyboard, use photos of the student's presentation. Get students to re-write the story of what happened to Breck. • Once work is complete, discuss with students that you are going to send their work to the Breck Foundation @breckfoundation (on social media) to show how the students have taught others about the Breck story. After this evaluate with students everything they have learnt over the previous weeks: • Good and bad computing and the internet; • Trusted people and why we have them; • Feelings that may come when things go wrong • Finally remind the students that what happened to Breck is extremely rare, however we are trying to keep as many people safe as possible. Remind them that this was a real story and that if any of the students have any worries, they must talk to a trusted adult.	• Please adapt the writing in the books to the size or symbol that is suitable to your class group • Appendix 13 can also be drawn by the students • If Appendix 13 is not suitable, you may want to create a poster for the Breck foundation, or a photo montage of the students work.	• Permission for students images to be used on social media • Camera • Appendix 13 • Images or video of the students presentation • Glue • Scissors BRECK FOUNDATION

Identified Opportunities for ICT: Any or all parts of this scheme of work can be transferred to computer. Please feel free to adapt and change to fit the needs of your students.

Helping the Breck Foundation: Please share with us any work, presentations, assemblies, work and displays that students create. Please make sure that you have all necessary permissions before sending anything to us. Please share with us on our social media @breckfoundation or email one of the team. We are developing our resources continually and like to see what ideas you come up with when sharing the story. Please look on our website for further resources and information, including videos, music and ways to support the foundation further. www.breckfoundation.org

Appendix 1

Letter to Parents and guardians regarding the intoduction to 'Breck and the Online Troll'

Dear Parent or Guardian

Over the next six weeks your child will be studying online safety and online grooming. We will be using the book 'Breck and the Online Troll' as our educational focus.

This book will introduce students to online grooming and issues surrounding internet safety. It is based on the true story of Breck Bednar. Breck was a 14-year-old boy who was groomed online whilst gaming with a person Breck belived was his friend. Breck was lured to the 18-year-old predator's flat and murdered.

Over the coming weeks your child may have further questions and may want to discuss what happened to Breck. There are lots of interviews and information online and on social media about Breck, and you may want to filter what is seen and read by your child.

We recommend that the book 'Breck and the Online Troll' is a good place to start when discussing this topic. A storybook edition is available to order online and and you can find out more information about Breck and the work of the charity, the Breck Foundation, at www.breckfoundation.org.

I will be arranging a meeting with parents and guardians on ____________________________ to discuss this scheme of work. Please let me know if you are able to attend or have any further questions.

We thank you for your continued support.

Regards

Appendix 2

Picture of the real Breck Bednar in Year 9

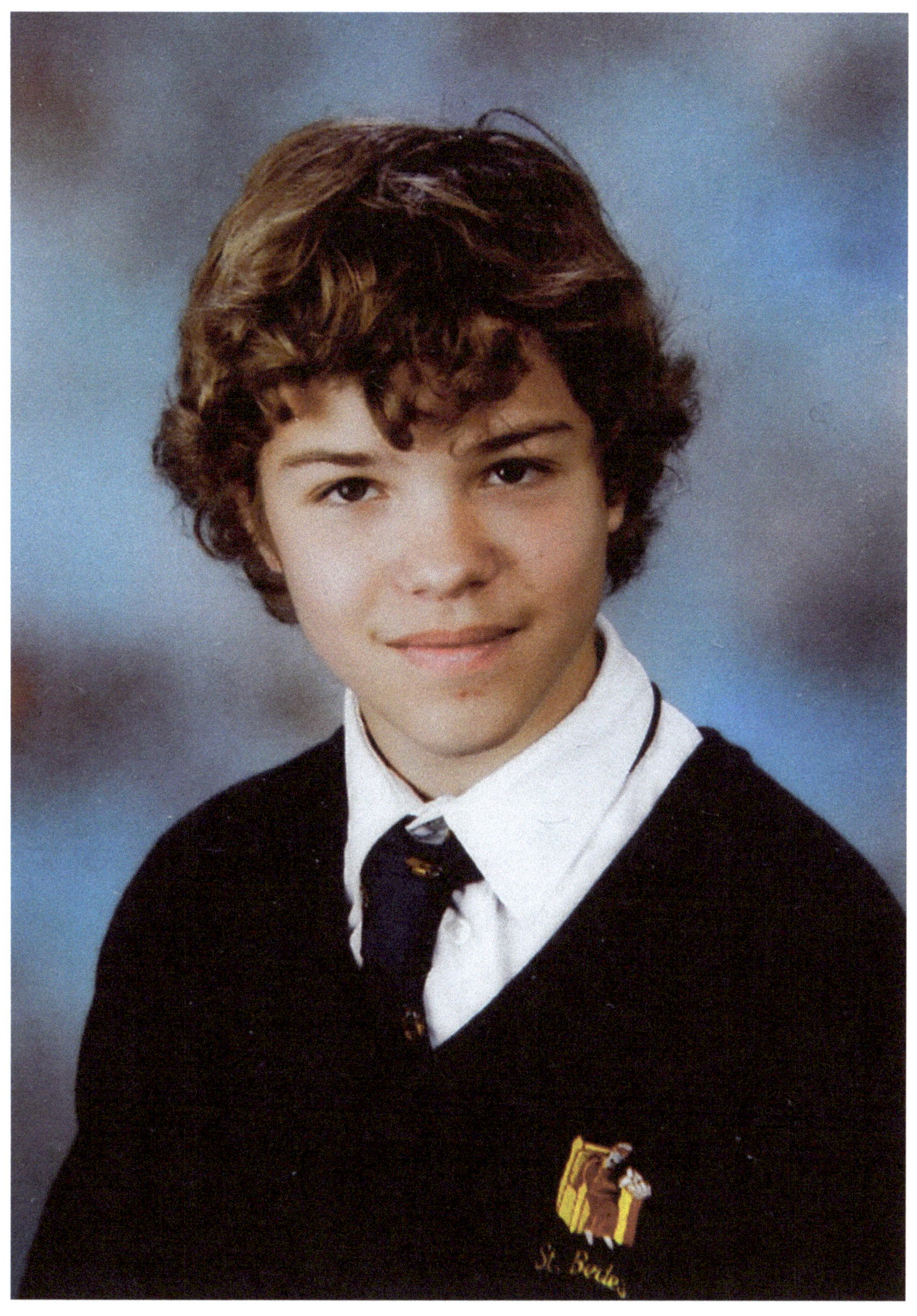

Appendix 3

'Fake news and True story.'

Fake news	True story

Appendix 4

Sentences for 'Fake News and True Story'

Breck was a real person	Breck was killed by a dragon	Lewis was a troll
Lewis was a real person	Lewis lied to Breck	Breck was a knight
Lewis had lots of money	Lewis killed Breck	Breck's mum was worried about Breck
Lewis didn't care about Breck	Breck was groomed by Lewis	Lewis didn't know what he was doing

Appendix 5

People I can talk to if I am worried.

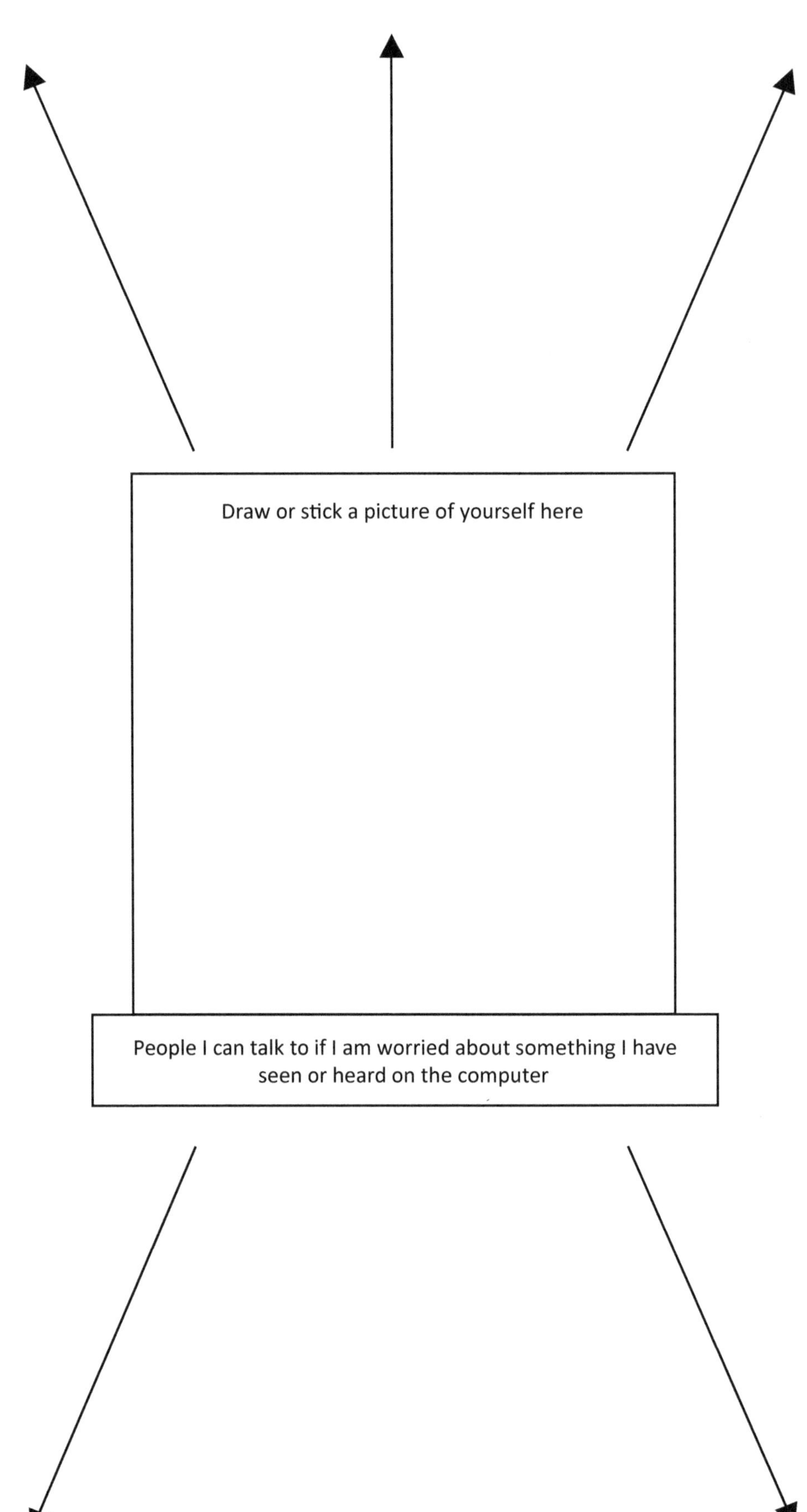

Appendix 6

List of people

Mum	Dad	Brother
Sister	Grandparents	Doctor
Teacher	Teaching Assistant	Police Officer
Social Worker	Carer	Auntie/Uncle
Shop Assistant	The lady next to you on the bus	Your friend

Appendix 7

Good and bad things about computing and the internet

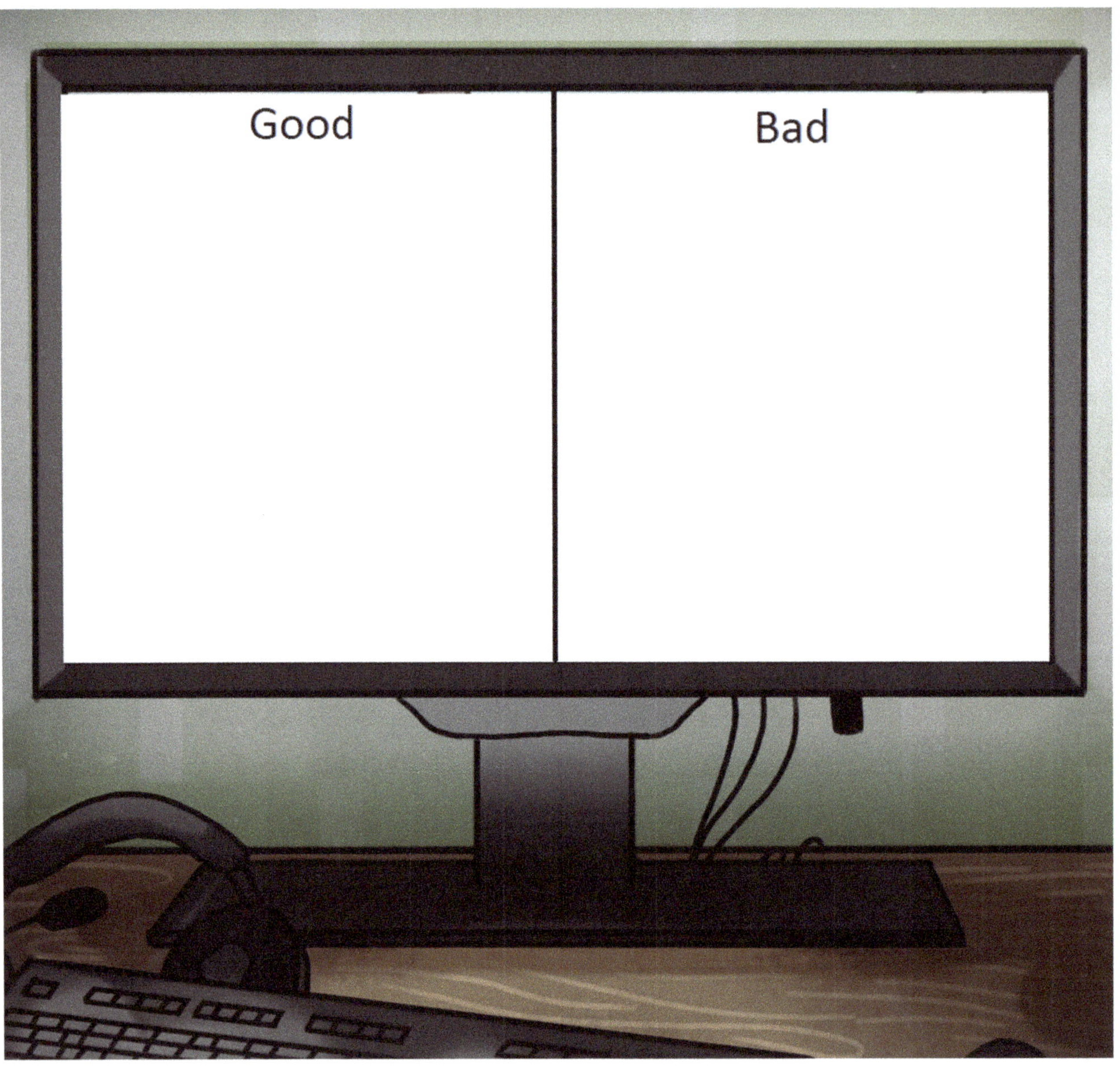

Appendix 8

Words for Good and Bad computing and the internet

Gaming with people you don't know	Doing work	Keeping in contact with friends and family
Speaking to people you don't know	Arranging to meet with people you don't know	Sending pictures to someone you don't know
Doing homework	Watching videos	Listening to music
Finding out information	Videos that are inappropriate	Spending a lot of time online online
Cyber-bullying	Doing something you know is wrong	Grooming

Appendix 9

What is grooming?

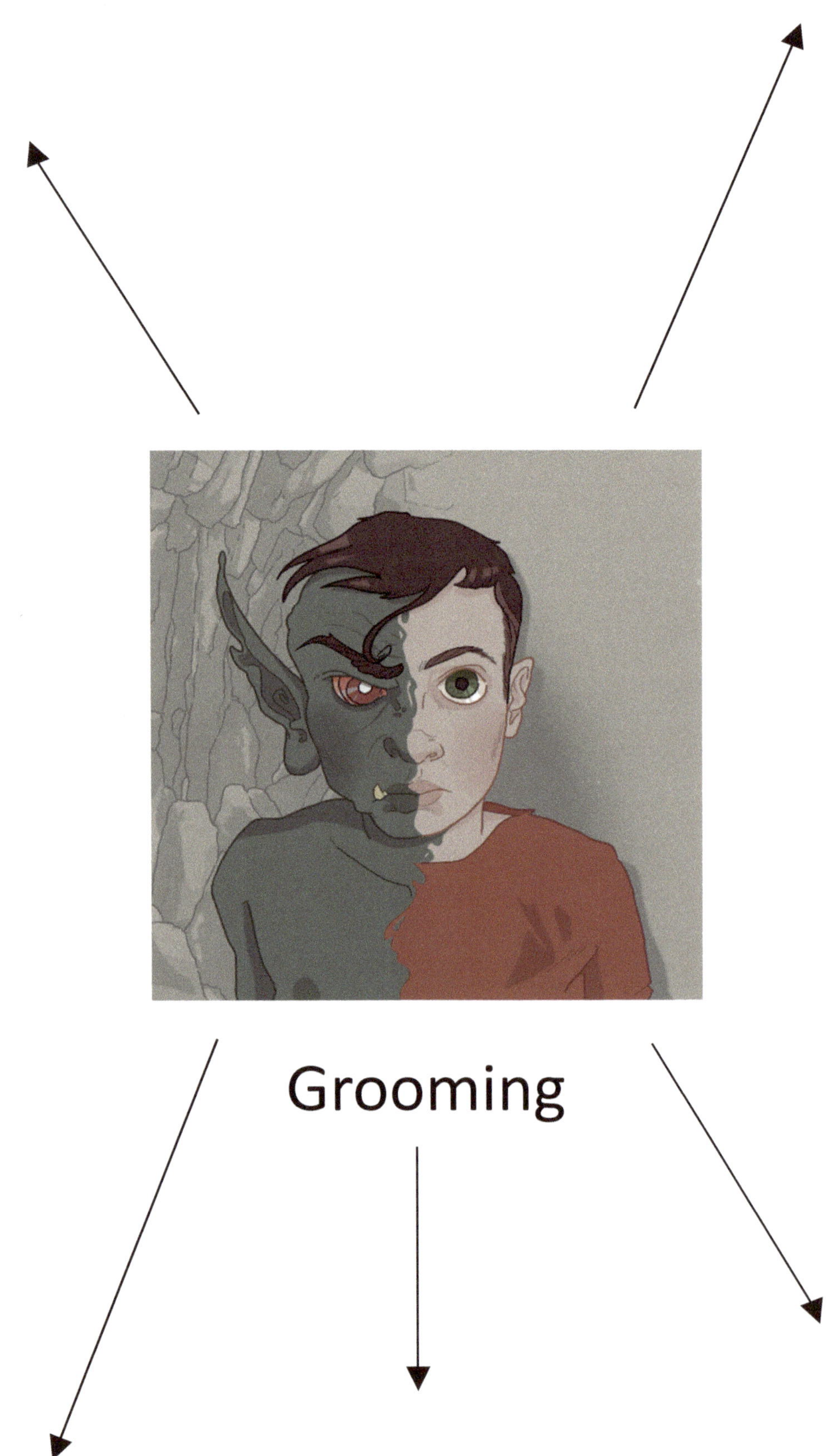

Appendix 10

Grooming sentence ideas

Pretends to have the same interest	Can be someone you know	Is only old people
A groomer can be any age	Only men groom people	Only females groom people
Anyone can be a groomer	At the start grooming feels good for the victim	Grooming someone can get you arrested
Grooming can affect your whole family	Grooming can change who you are	Groomers can use your emotions against you
Groomers can use your dreams against you	Groomers can hide their real identity	Groomers can pretend to be your friend.

Appendix 11

How might they feel?

Breck's Mum (Lorin)	Lewis
Breck	You (stick a picture of yourself here)

Appendix 12

Feelings

Sad	Angry	Confused
Lost	Happy	Lonely
Controlling	Mean	Excited
Trusted	Awful	Manipulative
Powerful	Tired	Manipulated

Appendix 13

Storyboard

www.ingramcontent.com/pod-product-compliance
Lightning Source LLC
LaVergne TN
LVHW070533110826
845147LV00017BA/984

* 9 7 8 1 9 1 3 6 3 0 7 0 6 *